Life for the World

Life for the World

A Way of Eucharistic Adoration for Today

by Marie Paul Curley, FSP

Pauline

BOOKS & MEDIA

Boston

Library of Congress Cataloging-in-Publication Data

Curley, Marie Paul.
  Life for the world : a way of eucharistic adoration for today / by
Marie Paul Curley.
      p. cm.
  ISBN 0-8198-4499-3 (pbk.)
  1. Lord's Supper—Adoration—Prayer-books and devotions—
English. 2. Alberione, James, 1884–1971. 3. Lord's Supper—
Adoration. I. Title.
  BX2233 .C87 2003
  264'.02036—dc21

                                        2002015650

The Old Testament Scripture quotations contained herein are from the *New Revised Standard Version Bible,* copyright © 1989 by the Division of Christian Education of the National Council of the Churches of Christ in the U.S.A. Used by permission. All rights reserved.

Except where noted, the texts of the Gospels used in this work are taken from *The Alba House Gospels,* translated by Mark A. Wauck, copyright © 1992 by the Society of St. Paul, Staten Island, New York, and are used by permission. All rights reserved.

Cover photo: Mary Emmanuel Alves, FSP

Art credit: Part Two, page 32—*The Washing of Feet,* © Sieger Köder, Fußwaschung.

Photo credits: Part One, page 2—Mary Emmanuel Alves, FSP; Part Three, page 138—FSP Photo Archives

Printed and published in the U.S.A. by Pauline Books & Media, 50 Saint Pauls Avenue, Boston MA 02130-3491.

www.pauline.org

Pauline Books & Media is the publishing house of the Daughters of St. Paul, an international congregation of women religious serving the Church with the communications media.

1 2 3 4 5 6 7   08 07 06 05 04 03

Gratefully dedicated to

Sr. Mary Veritas Grau, FSP

who helped me
discover the joy and excitement
of following the Master

Contents

Part One
"Way, Truth, and Life"

Part Two
"Come to Me"

Part Three
Popular Eucharistic Prayers

Part One

"Way, Truth, and Life."

Invitation

Perhaps you are looking for a way to deepen your relationship with God. You yearn for "something more", or you struggle with an emptiness deep inside. You are not alone in your search. God is not only aware of your deepest desires, but longs for a more intimate relationship with you. Many people have found healing, wholeness, and fulfillment by praying in the presence of the Eucharistic Jesus. The gift of the Eucharist is an amazing manifestation of God's great desire to be close to you. Deepening your connection with Jesus in the Eucharist is a special way to grow closer to the Lord who loves you so much.

There are two ways we worship Jesus in the Eucharist: by actively participating in the Eucharistic Celebration and by Eucharistic adoration. While the focus of this book is primarily Eucharistic adoration, it is important to begin with an understanding of how adoration flows from the Eucharistic Celebration.

The Perfect Prayer

For Christians, the Eucharist "is the source and summit" of life, the highest form of prayer.[1] The Eucharistic

Celebration defines us as Christians, uniting us to Christ, and through Christ to the Father. By participating in the Eucharistic Celebration weekly or even daily, we fulfill Christ's command, "Do this in memory of me," and gradually allow the saving power of Christ's love to touch every minute, every aspect of our lives.

The Eucharistic Celebration takes place within the Christian community, the People of God assembled together. There, we are invited to involve ourselves intimately in this sacrament of salvation. We are the People of God acting in union with Christ, and the Eucharistic Celebration is our most profound worship. From the Eucharist we celebrate, we are sent forth to take Christ's saving message to a world thirsting for God's love, justice, peace, and true freedom.

Living the Eucharist More Fully

While the Eucharistic Celebration is an act of worship we make together as the People of God, sometimes we need more time to reflect on the meaning of the Eucharist in our lives. The Church has long recognized the importance of private prayer and in a particular way has encouraged the faithful to pray in the presence of the Blessed Sacrament. Eucharistic adoration is a privileged time to ponder the tremendous mystery of Christ's self-giving love that we celebrate at Mass. Adoring Jesus in the Eucharist draws us deeper into the Paschal Mystery, strengthening our desire to share in the death and resurrection of the Lord.

Private adoration of Christ in the Eucharist is not a substitute for the Mass, but a way to deepen our living of the Eucharistic Celebration in all its fullness. Our adoration should lead us back to the Eucharistic Celebration, better prepared to appreciate its meaning and beauty. We can more readily recognize the fullness of the presence of Christ in the Word of God, in the presider, in the community, and in the Eucharistic bread and wine in which we receive the Body and Blood of Christ in Communion.

Invitation to Wholeness

Eucharistic adoration is a privileged time for those who seek to deepen their life in Christ. Maybe you are curious about Eucharistic adoration, but are not sure if it is for you or how to begin doing it. Or you may already spend time in prayer before the Blessed Sacrament occasionally, but you want to make this special prayer-time more meaningful. *Life for the World* is both an introduction to Eucharistic adoration and the presentation of a holistic method of adoration developed by a priest, Blessed James Alberione. Alberione's method offers a simple, Christ-centered structure for Eucharistic adoration that is valuable for both the beginner and the experienced.

In today's society, the need to integrate all the aspects of our lives is perhaps even more timely than it was a century ago when Alberione began developing his spirituality. We have all experienced times when our thoughts can lead us one way, while our feelings pull us another.

We tend to ignore our feelings or act against our better judgment instead of letting our actions take into account both what we feel and what we think.

Father Alberione's integrative and holistic approach to spirituality seriously challenges this tendency to break up our lives and stuff the fragments into separate compartments where they never relate to each other. Between work and home, church and school, public life and personal life, we often hide our true feelings and play different roles depending on where and with whom we find ourselves. We are embarrassed or even ashamed of certain aspects of ourselves that we take care to hide from others. In the face of this fragmentation, Alberione's spirituality is a welcome invitation to integration and wholeness. Jesus invites us to drop our masks in front of him and, in the comfort of his love, to come to appreciate and respect our deepest, truest selves. In the security of his love, we can open ourselves to the transforming power of his grace in all the areas of our lives, so that we can gradually become ever more faithful instruments of his love for transforming the world.

Pauline Spirituality

Blessed James Alberione (1884–1971), was an Italian priest who understood the value of Eucharistic adoration. He founded five active religious congregations, personally directed them, and guided their work.[2] In addition he founded four secular institutes.[3] His hectic schedule would seem to have left little room for adoration, yet he daily spent four to five hours in prayer before the Blessed Sacrament. He often called the hour of adoration one of the most fruitful and formative spiritual practices, because it allows for personal assimilation of the richness of the Eucharistic Celebration: "From this vital source, the Eucharistic Master, everything is given life."[4] "[The hour of adoration] prepares one for Holy Mass and Holy Communion. Frequent encounters and familiar conversation with Jesus produce friendship, resemblance, and identity of thought, of feeling, and of willing with Jesus."[5]

At the heart of Father Alberione's Eucharistic adoration lay his total preoccupation with the person of Christ. Father Alberione called the hour of adoration "the school of Jesus Master," comparing it to the time the first disciples spent coming to know, love, and follow the loving Teacher who called them. He also sometimes referred to the hour of adoration as "the Visit," an expression which signifies the intimate and intensely personal nature of this prayer.

Father Alberione developed a special Christ-centered way of making the hour of adoration. His method, known as the Pauline method because of Alberione's deep devotion to Saint Paul, is described in this book because it is easy to use and particularly relevant for today in its rich use of Scripture, its flexibility, and its holistic approach. The Pauline method encourages reading and reflecting on Scripture in each hour of adoration. The flexible structure allows for many prayer styles—both more active forms of prayer and genuine contemplation. The holistic approach of the Pauline method also challenges the individual to be receptive to the transforming action of God's Word in his or her attitudes, choices, and life.

It is easiest to understand the Pauline method of Eucharistic adoration in the light of the spirituality in which it is rooted.

Jesus Master

The Pauline spirituality is scripturally based, a synthesis of some of the richest passages in the New Testament, particularly in the Gospels and the Pauline letters. Beginning with the disciples' initial experience of Jesus as "Teacher" or "Master" in the Gospel, Father Alberione chose the word "Master" to describe the personal and unique relationship Jesus has with each of his disciples.[6] However, the term "master" has some negative associations that may make it seem unattractive; for example, master versus slave. The connotations of this usage are ownership, lordship, domination, and abusive power over others. But Jesus overturns our understanding of mastery and power in a stunning reversal: "You call me 'The Teacher' and 'The Lord,' and rightly so, because I am. If I, the Lord and Teacher, have washed your feet, you, too, ought to wash each other's feet" (John 13:13–14).

Jesus gave the term "master" a whole new meaning. Jesus is Master in order to serve. His lordship over us empowers us to live with the dignity of children of God. Jesus has definitively revealed the Father's love to us and committed himself to us. Through Jesus, we receive the full freedom and dignity of friendship with God. The mastery of Jesus Christ is that of perfect, complete, unconditional love. As our true Master, Jesus is the One who gives the deepest meaning to our lives, and we are his inasmuch as we were loved into being through him, he died to save us, and he constantly reveals his loving care for us.

This new meaning of the term "master" can be enriched by two other familiar connotations, the most immediate of which is "teacher."[7]

A teacher or master in the fullest sense does not just teach about one subject. A teacher's greatest impact on a student is the witness of his or her life, combined with the personal care and attention given to the student. Think of Yoda guiding Luke Skywalker in *Star Wars,* or Robin Williams as a high school teacher in *Dead Poets Society.* Such a mentor shares not only knowledge, but values and attitudes that will ultimately change the student's life.

The Divine Master's preaching constantly invites hearers of all times to a change of heart. But Jesus transforms the lives of his disciples above all by his relationship with them: the invitation to a very special intimacy with himself and with the Father.

Besides being understood as teacher, the term "master" can also be understood as guide. The ideal guide is an expert in a particular field who helps those following to reach the goal both safely and effectively. How invaluable a tour guide can be to those sightseeing in an unfamiliar country, or how irreplaceable the guidance of a coach when one is developing an artistic or athletic skill. As the ideal guide, Jesus does not just point us in a certain direction and leave it at that, but he is also a model. Jesus has walked the way himself and now accompanies us on every step of our journey, in both joyful and painful times.

Therefore, we understand Jesus as Master in light of the new meaning that Jesus himself gave to the term: Jesus is Master in the sense of servant, empowering the disciples to live in the fullness of freedom and love. Jesus Master still accompanies disciples of all time throughout their lives, teaching us through his Word, but even more by the witness of his life, his love for us, his guiding presence; in other words, by his relationship with us. As disciples, we share both in his life and in his call to serve.

Way, Truth, and Life

Father Alberione focused on several scriptural passages to "mine" the depth of the meaning of the term "Jesus Master." Deeply devoted to Saint Paul, Father Alberione focused on the heart of Saint Paul's teaching, which can be summed up in the Pauline expressions of what it means to have a relationship with Jesus: "It is no longer I who live, it is Christ who lives in me!" (Galatians 2:20) and "For me, to live is Christ" (Philippians 1:21). Father Alberione placed this Pauline concept of a central and vital relationship with Jesus in the context of Christ's profound self-definition, "I am the Way and the Truth and the Life" (John 14:6). The inspired genius of Father Alberione saw these distinct elements as intrinsically related to each other: We are invited to a personal relationship with Jesus Master who calls us to live in him and who becomes our Way, Truth and Life.[8]

Thus the heart of Alberione's Pauline spirituality can be summed up in this one phrase: Jesus Master, Way, Truth and Life; and it is as Way, Truth and Life that Jesus profoundly influences anyone who encounters him. Father Alberione saw Jesus' self-definition coinciding with the three essential aspects of each person: mind, will and heart. Alberione also believed that it is through Jesus Master, Way, Truth and Life, that the various aspects of the person could be integrated in a balanced, holy, and holistic way. According to Alberione's intuition, Jesus sanctifies the mind by revealing the deepest Truth about God and the person, the will by being the Way to happiness, and the heart by offering the eternal Life which we yearn for.

Jesus, the Truth that Sets Us Free

The terms "Jesus Master" and "Truth" seem particularly linked. It is easy to see that Jesus the Divine Master teaches us important truths so that we can live a happy and holy life. But Jesus' simple statement, "I am…the Truth" (John 14:6) does not just say he reveals truth; Jesus calls himself Truth. If we take his words seriously, we believe that Jesus is the ultimate Truth, the Answer to every question, the Revelation of God, the Promise that our life always has meaning.

Jesus is the Truth because it is in his very Person that we discover the mysterious reality of God: Love emptying itself completely for the sake of the Beloved. Jesus does more than tell us what the Father is like; he reveals the very face of God to us by entering into relationship with us.

The radical truth that God loves us unconditionally and wants to be in relationship with us is too powerful to just talk about: it has to be experienced. Perhaps this is why Jesus says, "I am Truth." Jesus not only reveals that God is our loving Father, but he unfolds for us the meaning of life and death, of joy and suffering, and of our own personal experience of the mystery of human existence. When we begin to accept Jesus as the truth of existence and of our very lives, we begin to recognize and take responsibility for our indestructible freedom and dignity as beings made in the image of God. Acknowledging and committing to the truth is the response of faith that Jesus asks of us. Faith in Jesus can transform our lives.[9]

Freedom is the ultimate consequence of accepting Jesus as Truth, but that acceptance is not always easy. The revelation of the truth may challenge some of the assumptions upon which we have based our lives. Discovering the truth or applying it to a real situation in our lives challenges our perceptions, our attitudes, our very understanding of reality and the choices we make. As we change, we influence the lives of those around us. It is not enough to pray for knowledge, we also need to pray for insight and the grace to accept and integrate the truth into our lives. In this regard, Father Alberione prayed, "Jesus Master, sanctify my mind, increase my faith."[10]

Jesus' words, his teaching, his incarnation, life, death and resurrection, and the ongoing teaching of his Spirit-guided Church are radiant truths that most clearly reveal the mystery of God and our relationship with God. Jesus is the Ultimate Truth every human person searches for. The saving truth of Christ is desperately needed in our world today. We are called to proclaim through our lives and witness that in Jesus Christ, the Son of God made man, the fullness of salvation is offered to every human being.[11]

Living our call to witness and proclaim this truth in our lives is a struggle. We do not need to be afraid, however: Jesus is with us in the struggle. Not only is he our Truth, he is also our Way.

Jesus, Way to the Father

At the Last Supper Jesus said, "I am the Way" to invite his disciples to follow him as the Way to the Father. In other places in the Gospel, Jesus offers himself as our model: "Learn from me" (Matthew 11:29), "I have given you an example so that, just as I have done for you, you, too, should do" (John 13:15), "Love one another as I have loved you" (John 15:13). Jesus invites us to contemplate him as our Way, and to live as he did.[12]

Because Jesus has shared the fullness of our human existence, his words, example, and entire life have a meaning that each of us can identify with. Father James Alberione prayed, "Master, Your life traces out the way for me... The manger, Nazareth, Calvary—all trace out the divine way."[13] These moments of Jesus' life are all poignantly human: both the joy and the stark poverty of a birth in a stable, the happy but also hard and simple life of the family of a poor carpenter, Jesus' agonizing death witnessed by his loving mother. Jesus is our Way because of the incarnation.

By his incarnation, Jesus united himself with every person, and by his suffering, death, and resurrection, he sought to bring each person to the fullness of life. Jesus lived the perfect life, not because it made sense according to society's standards or because he had everything his way, but because he lived his Father's will fully. By trusting completely in the Father's loving plan and by actively cooperating with God in every aspect of his life, Jesus showed us how to be the Father's beloved sons and daughters.

As his disciples, all of us are called to follow Jesus by way of the commandments and the beatitudes and, above all, by his new commandment of love. Jesus shows us the way to the Father by the example of his life, by his words in the Gospel, by the teaching of the Church, and by the lived experience of the People of God.

Accepting Jesus as our Way means that we make his priorities our own. However, the call to imitate Jesus doesn't require us to ignore our individuality, but to be uniquely happy, fulfilled, true to ourselves, and respectful of the image of God within us and others. Jesus, the face of God for us, acts with each of us individually, respecting our freedom, yet always seeking to bring us to deeper union with the Father. The respect and love that Jesus has for us are, perhaps, the first ways that we can imitate our Divine Model.

In the Gospels, whenever Jesus encountered someone, his first words were often questions addressing their needs or concerns, such as: "What do you seek?" or "What do you want me to do for you?" Jesus understood that each person is unique, having his or her own qualities, experiences, and needs. God created each of us as we are and gave each of us our own way of being. Because each of us is unique, we will each walk a unique path to God. It is first of all through our own being and experience that God calls us. God not only takes into account our history and personality, but builds on our strengths and invites us to let him transform our weaknesses.

It is not easy to be a true follower of Christ: We are called to imitate Jesus' selflessness and loving example. By ourselves, we might simply give up. But Jesus asks us to trust that his grace will sustain us and that he himself will be with us. Jesus does not leave us to walk alone; while we seek to follow his footsteps, we are often surprised to discover that he is walking beside us. The more attentive we are, the more frequently we discover his presence in our lives.

As we more closely follow Jesus Master, we discover that Jesus is both the Way to the Father and the Way to wholeness. We gradually learn how to balance the various aspects of our lives, living according to his values, which have become our priorities. We learn to genuinely love both ourselves and others; we discover that we are never alone; and we live out our Christian vocation in its deepest sense—as an active presence of God in the world.

The more closely we strive to follow Jesus, the deeper our longing grows for the fullness of love and life that only Jesus gives.

Jesus, Life for the World

Jesus used many images to talk about the life he brings to the world: flowing water, bread, salt, light, etc. There are, of course, as many meanings in Jesus' definition, "I am…Life" as there are in "I am…Truth" and "I am…Way."

The foundational belief of Christianity is that Jesus Christ, the God-Man, is our Redeemer—the One who became man, suffered, died, and rose to save us from death and bring us to everlasting life. Jesus saves us in innumerable ways: from original sin, from our personal sins and sinfulness, from social sinfulness, and from evil in the world around us. This belief is the core of the Christian faith, and it is meant to be experienced by every Christian in a very personal way.

In saving us, Jesus offers a priceless gift that is unimaginable to the non-believer: sharing in his own life. "I am the vine, you are the branches. Whoever abides in me, and I in him, he it is who bears much fruit" (John 15:5). Jesus invites us to union with him: to participate in the very life of God. That is why the sacraments, beginning with Baptism, and preeminently the Eucharist, are such incredible gifts. They enable Christians to enter into and nourish within themselves the very life of God.[14]

Jesus said, "I have come that you might have life and have it abundantly" (John 10:10). He used images of nature's generous extravagance, such as "living water" and "living bread," to describe the fullness of life he offers. To truly live in Christ means experiencing the fullness of human life: a deeper love, freedom, joy and fulfillment, and sometimes a deeper grief in suffering. A genuine Christian life entails a profound sharing in the Paschal Mystery. Jesus calls every disciple to share uniquely in the mystery of his passion, death, and resurrection. To the believer, every form of death can be a passageway to new life, because although God does not directly will evil, God can bring good through even the most tragic circumstance. In the experience of suffering, the disciple is consoled and strengthened both by the presence of Jesus and by Jesus' promise of resurrection and new life.

As Jesus' self-giving love transforms us, we realize we are called to love others in that same selfless way: "Love one another as I have loved you" (John 15:12). As disciples of the Master we are to share in his love and concern for each person. This call to love often means sacrifice; certainly it is another way we share in the Paschal Mystery with Jesus. To love as Jesus does often requires a sometimes painful reshaping of our hearts to be more like his.

Union with Jesus is not a static experience meant just for the individual's consolation. Genuine union with Jesus in prayer is ongoing: Jesus shares his life with us in a way that impacts our entire being, even if we don't feel anything special. We gradually become aware of how Jesus is calling us to be his hands, his words, and his heart for everyone we meet, live with, and work with.

Jesus gives himself to us in the Eucharist in order to share his life with us, and through us, with the world. A true encounter with the Master kindles a new passion within. Alight with the love of Christ, the disciple wants to share that light with everyone. A preeminent example is Saint Paul, whose conversion from persecutor to apostle of Christianity completely changed the history of the early Church. As the fullness of God's life explodes within us and transforms us, we are impelled to radiate God's love towards others. Jesus wants to work through us to accomplish his mission, and he gives us the joy and energy to respond generously to his call.

In short, Pauline spirituality is all about developing a personal relationship with Jesus Master who is our Way, Truth, and Life. Jesus not only proclaims the truth, but is himself the Truth because it is in him that we discover the face of God. Jesus shows us the Way to the Father by the example he gave in living among us, but also by walking with us on our journey. As our Life, Jesus saves us from the darkness of sin and invites us to the deepest possible fulfillment by sharing in the mystery of his life, death, and resurrection. When we enter more deeply into relationship with Jesus, Way, Truth, and Life, we discover that our daily life begins to change and grow. Our relationship with the Lord begins to impact our relationship with others and with the world itself.

Way, Truth, and Life for the World

Pauline spirituality never leaves one in the comfort of a quiet chapel or the complacency of a self-centered life, but compels us to live the Gospel fully in our own lives. As we come to know, love, and follow Jesus Master, Way, Truth, and Life, we hear his invitation to become way, truth, and life for our world today. In light of this, two more Scripture passages are key in the Alberionian understanding of Jesus Master.

One passage is: "Come to me, all you grown weary and burdened, and I will refresh you. Take my yoke upon you and learn from me, for I am gentle and humble hearted and you will find rest for your souls" (Matthew 11:28 – 29).

"Come to me" is Jesus' invitation to all of us, drawing us to himself. Jesus yearns to be an intimate part of our lives, to refresh us and hold us, to give us the fulfillment we seek. In this invitation, Jesus describes the perfect attitude for making an hour of adoration: to let go of our burdens, to listen, and to be transformed by him. These words can be seen as a direct invitation to each of us to visit Jesus in the Eucharist.

The other passage is a mandate: "Go, therefore, and make disciples of all nations, baptizing them in the name of the Father and of the Son and of the Holy Spirit, and teach them to observe all that I've commanded you, and behold I'll be with you all the days until the end of the age" (Matthew 28:19–20). Jesus sends those who have encountered him to actively witness to him in their lives. He wants us to be his presence in the world today.

"Come to me" and "Go!" might seem contradictory, but they are really two spiritual movements of the heart. Jesus calls us to ever deeper union with himself, and he also calls us to greater witness of life and love for one another. The more we witness to Christ, the more we feel the need to be intimately united to him. Likewise, the more we glimpse the face of Christ in prayer, the more clearly we hear the urgent call to proclaim him, whether in some form of ecclesial ministry or by loving service, especially to the poor, the suffering, and victims of injustice.

The Pauline Hour of Adoration

Now that we are familiar with the basics of Pauline spirituality on which Father Alberione based his method of Eucharistic adoration, we turn to the hour of adoration itself. The method of making a Pauline hour of adoration and its simple structure follows the three-fold definition Jesus gave himself—as Way, Truth, and Life.

The hour of adoration is divided into three "moments," or parts. It may be helpful especially for beginners to divide the hour into three segments of approximately twenty minutes each. But a rigid time constraint is not important; what is essential is that time be given to each of these three moments. In the first part, we adore Jesus, listening attentively to his Word to us today and letting his Truth shape our minds and attitudes. In the second part, we contemplate Jesus as our Way and Model, and the practical consequences of his loving presence in our lives. In the third part, we try to open our hearts completely to Jesus Life, to let his sustaining grace and peace touch our hearts so that we can bring that same peace and love to others.

The hour of adoration begins by becoming attentive to the presence of God. We try to slow our minds, seeking to focus our attention on God and on this particular time. We open our hearts to the loving appeal of Jesus, "Come to me…." A hymn or prayer of adoration is a good way to enter into a prayerful spirit.

Adoring Jesus Truth

After a hymn or prayer of adoration, we choose or remind ourselves of the theme of the hour if we have one, or we ask for a particular grace. The chosen theme or the grace that we ask for becomes a recurring motif throughout the hour of adoration.

Then we ask the light of the Holy Spirit to enlighten and nourish us as we prepare to listen to the Word of God. We read a passage of Scripture, chosen according to the theme, and adore Jesus in his Word. We listen attentively, not only with our ears but also with our hearts, letting Jesus Truth enlighten us and give us new understanding and insight. The Word of God is powerful; when we let it enter into our lives, it will not leave us untouched.

During the time that follows, we can reread and reflect, conversing with Jesus about how this Scripture passage touches our life and what it means for us today, in our situation. Adoring Jesus Truth through frequent reading of the Scriptures strengthens our faith and influences our attitudes. We gradually begin to see and experience life in the light of faith. In fact, faith is a special gift we can ask for during this first part of the hour—a faith that will transform us into more committed disciples of Jesus.

Although reading other material can be beneficial, the reading of Scripture is especially encouraged because Sacred Scripture is the Word of God—God truly speaks to us through the Scriptures. In the hour of adoration, we can take the time for that to happen. We may find that a very brief passage gives us a great deal to reflect on. On the other hand, we may find it more difficult to settle down or to reflect, and then it might be better to read until a passage sparks an insight. However much we read, it is most important to leave time for reflection, allowing Jesus' saving Word to enlighten us, here and now, where we are today.

We conclude this first part by responding to the Word of God with an act of faith, an affirmation of our belief in and our commitment to Christ. This act of faith, whether formal or spontaneous, prepares us to seek to follow Jesus more closely.

Following Jesus Way

Having just recommitted ourselves to Christ in the first part of the hour of adoration, in the second part we contemplate Jesus as our Way and our Model, and we look more closely at our relationship with him. Taking up the theme of the Scripture passage and our reflection, we contemplate God's action in our own lives. First, we thank God for the many and marvelous ways we have been touched by God's loving gifts. As we become aware of God's many blessings, we realize that we have often failed to respond to those blessings. We then confront our lives with Jesus' words and example.

Journaling can be a helpful tool in this regard, particularly by increasing our awareness of the Lord's action in our lives. Journaling in the form of a prayer can also enable us to enter more deeply into a prayerful spirit. Whether on paper or in spirit, we ask ourselves how Jesus is calling us to follow him more closely and how we need to change —in our attitudes, actions, or desires—so that we can become more like him. We try to imagine what Jesus would do in our place, and how we can draw closer to the Father. Then, we express our sorrow for our sinfulness and renew our resolve to more faithfully follow our loving Master in the concrete way we live our life.

Both thanksgiving and examining our conscience are important to this time of prayer. Without an appreciation of God's goodness to us, we cannot recognize how we have failed to respond to his call. Without recognizing our failures, our thanksgiving might be very superficial; God loves us in our weaknesses, not despite them.

As we turn to God in gratitude and humility, we realize that we do not have the strength to change on our own. But we can renew our trust that God will give us the graces we need to do so. Jesus wants us to trust in him. He wants us to be his presence in the world today. He will act powerfully in our lives as we strive to follow him more closely. Through this second part of the hour, we open ourselves to living in continual conversion.

Sharing Jesus' Life

Converted anew, we enter the third part of the hour of adoration ready for more intimate communication with Jesus as our Life, the source of grace, of strength, of union with the Father. United to Jesus Life, we contemplate his love for the Father, for all humanity, and for each of us. We become true apostles as we bring to God our own needs and the needs of the world. Prayers of petition, but also praise and contemplation of God's goodness, rise from our hearts. Whether this prayer is offered spontaneously or more formally in the form of the Rosary, the Stations, the Liturgy of the Hours, a psalm, or other prayers, we seek a union of love with Jesus Life, who poured out his life for us. We offer him our hearts in love in order to become completely one with him and to become communicators of his love to the world.

This is time for "prayer of the heart," that is, letting ourselves be loved by the Lord, sharing with God our needs and our deepest desires, and asking to be transformed into witnesses of his love and truth.

We conclude our hour of adoration with an act of love and return to daily life refreshed and renewed. As we share more fully in the life of Christ, we discover that as Jesus is Life for the world, so he calls us to be life for the world:

to bring the fullness of our life in Christ to the world in which we live and work.

Practical Notes on Using the Hours of Adoration in This Book

The hours of adoration offered here come from the rich tradition of Pauline spirituality. I hope they will enable you to make this beautiful and effective method of prayer your own. Times of adoration are meant to be intensely personal moments spent with our loving Master. The outlines given here are meant as suggestions or helps, but are to be used freely, according to your individual needs and desires.

The first three hours of adoration are presented in more detail so that the method will become clear, and also so that the hours can be easily used in a group as described below. The following nine hours of adoration are outlined, and the details are left to the creativity of the person praying and the inspiration of the Spirit.

The third part of the book is a collection of additional prayers that can be used during adoration. Several blank pages have been provided for you to include personal favorites.

In time, you will be able to go beyond the simple outlines provided here and confidently adapt the Pauline method for your own hours of adoration. As you become more accustomed to using this method for the hour of adoration, you may find that you have become so familiar with it that you spontaneously move from one part to the next without following the outline as it is presented here. For example, instead of making a particular prayer-response to the Scripture reading as initially suggested, you may find that the entire second part of the visit becomes your response. Or the divisions between the three parts gradually blur and merge as you move from reading to reflection to personal application to intense prayer.

The Pauline method can be invaluable in developing one's prayer life, but whenever we use a method in prayer, we want to be attentive to the Spirit's lead. It is the Spirit who prays within us and teaches us how to pray. The Spirit will help us enter into deeper union with Jesus, our Way, Truth, and Life, both during our hours of adoration and throughout our daily lives.

Adapting These Hours of Adoration for a Group

Many prayer groups make hours of adoration together. While a significant amount of silence should be included in any hour of adoration to allow for private prayer, many elements can be prayed together. Because these hours of adoration are intended for both individual and group prayer, some hours use the terms "me" and "my," and others use "we" and "our." As a group leader, you may wish to adapt the language so that it is more appropriate to the group.

Introduction

A group can begin by singing an appropriate hymn. The theme can be introduced aloud by the leader, and the prayer for enlightenment can be prayed together.

First Part of the Hour: Adoring Jesus Truth

The reading is best proclaimed aloud. Additional comments on the reading may be read either aloud or silently. However, time for silent reflection during this first part should always be included. At the conclusion, an act of faith may be made together in the form of reciting the Creed or another prayer, singing a hymn, etc.

Second Part of the Hour: Following Jesus Way

The leader can guide the group in offering thanks, possibly inviting individuals to share aloud their gratitude to God. The prayer of thanksgiving can be prayed together, using a hymn or prayer such as the Magnificat.

The examination of conscience may be introduced by a quotation or question that sets a direction for personal reflection, but ample silence here is usually the most helpful. The act of contrition and act of trust can be prayed aloud together. An appropriate hymn can help the group renew trust in the Lord and strengthen resolve to follow Jesus more closely.

Third Part of the Hour: Sharing Jesus Life

In the third part, prayer can either be silent or aloud. Members of the group can be invited to spontaneously express prayer intentions for themselves and for the world. The Rosary, the Stations, the Liturgy of the Hours, or individual psalms can easily be prayed together. Finally, the group may conclude their hour of adoration by singing a hymn that expresses a renewed commitment to living out the Gospel of love in their daily lives.

Part Two

"Come to Me"

HOUR OF 1 ADORATION

Encountering the Master

*To rediscover who Jesus is for me
at this moment in my life.*

Introduction and Prayer of Awareness

Lord, it is good to be here in your Eucharistic presence, to adore you, to be able to spend some privileged, intimate moments with you. I want to be fully present to you and really treasure this time with you.

Lord, I love you. And I want to know you better, as good friends desire to know more and more about each other. Knowing you better, I will love you more. I can never love you enough. Help me to discover what you would like our relationship to become.

Reveal yourself to me, and help me to be open and attentive to what you want to say to me in your Word to day.

Spend a few moments in silent adoration.

Adoring Jesus Truth

Ask the light of the Holy Spirit to illumine your mind and heart. In today's reading, Jesus asks the disciples to honestly tell him what they think of him. Is Jesus inviting you to a heart-to-heart conversation about your relationship with him? Read the following passage of Scripture slowly, pausing to ponder what impresses you.

Reading   Matthew 16:13–19

Now when Jesus came to the district of Caesarea Philippi he began to question his disciples, "Who do they say the Son of Man is?" So they said, "Some say John the Baptist, others, Elijah, still others, Jeremiah or one of the prophets." Then he asked them, "But *you*—who do *you* say I am?" Peter replied, "You're the Messiah, the Son of the Living God!" And in response Jesus said to him,

"Blessed are you, Simon son of Jonah,
For it was not flesh and blood that
    revealed this to you,
But my Father in Heaven.

And now *I* tell *you,* that you are Peter,
And on this rock I will build my church,
And the gates of Hell will not prevail against it.

I will give you the keys to the Kingdom of Heaven,
And whatever you bind on earth will have been
    bound in Heaven,

And whatever you loose on earth will have been
    loosed in Heaven."

Reflection

"Who do you say that I am?" Let this direct question
of Jesus penetrate your heart. Who is Jesus for you today?
Jesus constantly reveals himself to us in the Scriptures, in
the Eucharist, in our daily lives. Take a few moments to
reflect on your relationship with Jesus. By what name do
you usually call Jesus? What is the name of Jesus that is
most meaningful to you?

*After some minutes of reflection, pray the Litany to Jesus
Master as an act of faith in response to the reading, adding your own favorite title of Jesus at the end.*

Litany to Jesus Master

Jesus Master, Way, Truth and Life, *have mercy
    on me!*
Jesus, gentle Master, *increase my faith!*
Jesus Truth, Light of the world, *increase my faith!*
Jesus, Word of the Father, *increase my faith!*
Jesus, fulfillment of all my dreams, *increase
    my faith!*
Jesus, Light of my life, *increase my faith!*
Jesus, my Salt, *increase my faith!*
Jesus, Center of my life, *increase my faith!*

Jesus, Mystery of Love, *increase my faith!*
Jesus, who knows my inmost thoughts,
     increase my faith!
Jesus, present in the tabernacle,
     increase my faith!
Jesus, Revealer of the Father's love,
     increase my faith!
Jesus who gives meaning to every event
     in my life, *increase my faith!*
Jesus, my Inspiration, *increase my faith!*
Jesus, God beyond my imagination,
     increase my faith!
Jesus, Way to the Father, *I trust in You.*
Jesus, my Guide, *I trust in You.*
Jesus, Way for the lost, *I trust in You.*
Jesus, Model of holiness, *I trust in You.*
Jesus, Companion on the journey, *I trust in You.*
Jesus, my Security, *I trust in You.*
Jesus Master, who counts as precious all my tears,
     I trust in you.
Jesus, my Rock and Refuge, *I trust in You.*
Jesus, my unfailing Hope, *I trust in You.*
Jesus always with me, *I trust in You.*
Jesus, Partner in the dance of life, *I trust in You.*
Jesus, faithful Friend, *I trust in You.*
Jesus who shapes and molds me through
     life's daily situations, *I trust in You.*

Jesus on whom I lean, *I trust in You.*
Jesus, Good Shepherd, *I trust in You.*
Jesus, Joy of my life, *live in me.*
Jesus, unconditional Lover, *live in me.*
Jesus, life-giving Bread, *live in me.*
Jesus, ever-flowing Water, *live in me.*
Jesus my All, *live in me.*
Jesus, my Redeemer, *live in me.*
Jesus, my deepest Desire, *live in me.*
Jesus who died for me, *live in me.*
Jesus, healing Master, *live in me.*
Jesus, Transformer of hearts, *live in me.*
Jesus, my Beloved, *live in me.*
Jesus, gentle Listener, *live in me.*
Jesus, faithful beyond death, *live in me.*
Jesus, suffering with Your people, *live in me.*
Jesus, my Delight, *live in me.*
Jesus who calls me, *have mercy on me!*
Jesus who molds me, *have mercy on me!*
Jesus who challenges me, *have mercy on me!*
Jesus who sends me, *have mercy on me!*
Jesus Master, Way, Truth and Life, *have mercy
    on me!*

Following Jesus Way

In the Scripture reading from Matthew, Jesus gives
Simon a new name: Peter. You were given a "new" name

HOUR
1

when you were baptized, symbolizing your new relationship with God. Jesus continues to call you by name each day. Take a few moments to thank the Lord for the incredible gift of his relationship with you, perhaps focusing on one particular way in which you feel the Lord has shown his love to you. Perhaps it is a time when you felt the presence of Jesus very close to you; or perhaps it is a very special way God has blessed your life—by the Church, by a person, by a special opportunity.

After a suitable time of thanksgiving in your own words, you can unite it with Mary's thanksgiving, praying the Magnificat.

My soul gives praise to the Lord,
    and my spirit rejoices in God my Savior;
Because He had regard for the lowliness
      of His handmaid,
    behold, henceforth all generations shall
      call me blessed,
For the Mighty One has done great things for me,
    and holy is His name,
And His mercy is from generation to generation
    toward those who fear Him.
He has shown might with His arm,
    scattered the arrogant in the conceit
      of their heart,
He has pulled down the mighty from their thrones,
    and exalted the lowly,

The hungry He has filled with good things,
 and the rich He has sent away empty.

He has come to the aid of His servant, Israel,
 mindful of His mercy,
Just as He promised our fathers,
 Abraham and his descendants forever.

Luke 1:46–55

In listening to the Master's words and reflecting on Jesus' great love for you, have you heard Jesus inviting you to follow him more closely? Perhaps you see a way in which you have not responded to his love for you. Now is a good opportunity to bring to Jesus those situations in your life in which you find it difficult to hear or follow his call.

Pause to reflect on the challenges of your own life, confronting how you live with the words and example of Jesus.

Express your sorrow and trust in the Lord with an Act of Contrition.

My loving God,
I am sorry with all my heart
for the times I have acted out of sinfulness
 or weakness,
or when I have failed to act out of love.
You love me so much, yet I keep sinning
 against you,
whom I want to love above everything else.

HOUR
1

Have mercy on me and forgive me,
in the name of your Son, Jesus,
who died for us.
Strengthen me and help me not to sin anymore.
With your grace, I will try
to always live in your love.

Sharing Jesus' Life

The Scriptures, especially the psalms, are full of images of God—God is Rock, Inheritance, Strength, Maker, Builder, Shepherd. Choose one of your favorite psalms (or turn to the prayer section and pick a psalm there), or make up a psalm of your own that celebrates your relationship with God. Through the words of the psalm, take time to treasure the gift of your relationship with Jesus and the gift that your relationship with Jesus engenders for the world.

As a concluding prayer, pray the Psalm to the Divine Master *(based on Psalm 23).*

The Lord is my Master,
he teaches me the art of loving.
Most patient, he understands
the inner movements of my soul.
The Lord lights up my darkness.
Through all creation, he teaches me—
I will sit forever at his feet.

HOUR
1

He speaks softly within me,
leading me by my own heart.
Though I can't see the path,
his eyes never lose me.
Turning to him I am safe,
wrapt in the blanket of his Love.
He calls me to follow him more closely—
Clasping his nail-pierced hand.

My Master died and rose for me,
loving me into life.
He transforms every sadness.
His ever-present kindness and mercy
make each day shine anew.
I sing out my joy in him
and proclaim his abundant goodness—
he fills up my life.

*As you prepare to leave Jesus' Eucharistic presence, think
of one way that you can share with someone else the gift
that your relationship with Jesus has been for you.*

HOUR
1

Jesus the Good Shepherd

To trust more in Jesus as we follow him.

Prayer of Presence
by Venerable James Alberione

We adore you, Jesus,
eternal Shepherd of the human race.
You are present in the Eucharist
to dwell continually in the midst of your people.
You nourish us, you guard us,
you guide us to the heavenly fold.
We do not live on bread alone,
but on your Word of truth and love.
We listen to your voice
and follow it with love.
Give us the grace to listen to and love your Word,
that it may bear fruit in our hearts.
Speak, Lord, your servant is listening.

Spend a few moments in private adoration.

Adoring Jesus Truth

We ask the Holy Spirit to help us to be attentive to Jesus'
words to us today.

The Good Shepherd is a comforting image, represent-
ing God's fidelity and nurturing love for us. No matter
how we feel, Jesus is always with us on life's journey.

Reading   John 10:1–30

"Amen, amen, I say to you,

> Whoever doesn't go in by the gate
> into the sheepfold
> but enters by another way,
> he's a thief and robber.

> But whoever comes in by the gate,
> he's the shepherd of the sheep.
> The gatekeeper opens to him,
> and the sheep hear his voice,
> and he calls his own sheep by name, and leads
>   them out.

> When he drives out all his own sheep
> he goes before them,
> and the sheep follow him
> because they know his voice.

> But they don't follow a stranger,
> instead, they flee from him,
> because they don't know
> the voice of strangers."

Jesus told them this figure of speech, but they didn't realize what it was he was telling them.

So once again Jesus said, "Amen, amen, I say to you,

> I am the gate for the sheep!
> All those who came before me
>   are thieves and robbers,
> But the sheep didn't listen to them.
> I am the gate!
> Whoever comes in through me will be saved
> And will enter and leave and find pasture.
> The thief comes only to steal and slaughter
>   and slay;
> I've come that you might have life
>   and have it abundantly.
> I am the *good* shepherd;
> The good shepherd lays down his life
>   for his sheep.
> But since the hired man is not a shepherd—
>   the sheep are not his own—
> When he sees the wolf coming
>   he leaves the sheep and flees,
> And the wolf carries them off and scatters them,
> Because he's a hired man and doesn't care
>   about the sheep.
> I am the *good* shepherd,
> And I know mine and mine know me,
> Just as the Father knows me and I know
>   the Father,

HOUR
2

And I lay down my life for my sheep.
I have other sheep who are not of this fold,
    and I must lead them,
And they'll listen to my voice,
    and become one flock, one shepherd.
This is why the Father loves me,
Because I lay down my life in order to take
        it up again.
No one takes it from me;
On the contrary, I lay it down on my own.
I have power to lay it down and I have power
        to take it up again.
This is the command I've received
        from my Father."

Once again a split arose among the Jews because of these words. Now many of them said, "He has a demon and is out of his mind! Who can listen to him?" Others said, "These are not the words of a demon-possessed man! Can a demon open the eyes of the blind?"

At that time Hanukkah was taking place in Jerusalem. It was winter and Jesus was walking in the Temple in the Portico of Solomon. So the Jews surrounded him and said, "How long will you keep us in suspense? If you're the Messiah, tell us openly!" Jesus answered them,

"I told you and you don't believe.
The works I do in the name of my Father—
    these bear witness to me,

But you don't believe because you're not
   from among my sheep.
My sheep listen to my voice,
And I know them, and they follow me,
And I give them eternal life and they'll never die,
And no one will snatch them from my hand.
My Father, Who has given them to me,
   is greater than all,
And no one can snatch them
   from the hand of the Father.
The Father and I are one."

Reflection

This reading highlights many details about the relationship between a good shepherd and his sheep: The shepherd calls each sheep by name, personally leading them; the sheep recognize the shepherd's voice; the shepherd would willingly give his life to save his sheep. It's a warm, intimate picture of the trusting relationship between shepherd and sheep.

Jesus calls himself the Good Shepherd, who leads and accompanies us wherever we go. Jesus leads us to the Father, wanting to give us the fullness of life. What is the next step Jesus is asking us to take? Do we trust that the Lord will be with us? What are the obstacles that prevent us from stepping forward with Jesus?

As an act of faith, pray Psalm 100 that celebrates our relationship with God as our Shepherd.

HOUR
2

Psalm 100

Make a joyful noise to the LORD, all the earth.
    Worship the LORD with gladness;
    come into his presence with singing.

Know that the LORD is God.
    It is he that made us, and we are his;
    we are his people, and the sheep of his pasture.

Enter his gates with thanksgiving,
    and his courts with praise.
    Give thanks to him, bless his name.

For the LORD is good;
    his steadfast love endures forever,
    and his faithfulness to all generations.

Following Jesus Way

Read the following Parable of the Lost Sheep, picturing yourself as the lamb being picked up with joy by the Shepherd:

So he told them this parable, "What man among you who had a hundred sheep and lost one of them wouldn't leave the ninety-nine in the desert and set out after the lost one until he found it? And when he finds it he puts it on his shoulders, rejoicing, and when he comes home he calls his friends and neighbors together and says to them, 'Rejoice with me— I've found my lost sheep!' I say to you that, likewise, there will be more joy in Heaven at the repentance of one sinner than at ninety-nine of the righteous who had no need of repentance."

Luke 15:3–7

In what ways have you felt shepherded by God? Take a few minutes to express your gratitude. In what area(s) of your life do you feel lost or hurt? What do you feel unable to cope with or trust God about? God desires to embrace and heal you, even in your most hidden or wounded places. Can you bring these areas of your life to God?

Pause to reflect on the challenges of your life, confronting your life with the words and example of Jesus.

We express our sorrow and trust in the Lord.

To Jesus, the Good Shepherd
by Venerable James Alberione

We thank you, Jesus Good Shepherd,
for having come down from heaven
to seek out humankind
and bring us back to the way of salvation.
You are the Good Shepherd
who gathers and cares
for the scattered sheep.
The shepherd leads
and the sheep follow
because they recognize the shepherd's voice.

HOUR
2

You have given your commandments,
your counsels, your examples.
Whoever heeds them is nourished
with a bread that does not perish:
"My food is to do the will of the heavenly Father."
Have mercy on us when we try to nourish ourselves
on falsehood or empty pleasures.
Recall us to your way.
Sustain us when we waver,
    strengthen us when we are weak.
May everyone follow you,
Shepherd and Guardian of our souls.
You alone are the Way,
you alone have words of eternal life.
We will follow you wherever you go.

Sharing Jesus Life

Pray Psalm 23 slowly, using the psalm below, or the words of a favorite hymn based on Psalm 23. As we pray each phrase, pause to thank the Lord for shepherding us in that way in our lives. Or, if one phrase or line is particularly meaningful, repeat it slowly and let it become a reminder throughout the next day or week of God's goodness. Ask God to bring a deeper trust in God's love for you into your daily life.

(If praying together, the group can pause after each sentence and spontaneously offer aloud their thanksgiving.)

Psalm 23

The LORD is my shepherd, I shall not want.
    He makes me lie down in green pastures;
he leads me beside still waters;
    he restores my soul.
He leads me in right paths
    for his name's sake.

Even though I walk through the darkest valley,
    I fear no evil;
for you are with me;
    your rod and your staff—
    they comfort me.

You prepare a table before me
    in the presence of my enemies;
you anoint my head with oil;
    my cup overflows.
Surely goodness and mercy shall follow me
    all the days of my life
and I shall dwell in the house of the LORD
    my whole life long.

As we conclude the hour of adoration, we ask God to help us remember and reflect God's loving kindness for us throughout our day or week.

HOUR
2

HOUR OF ADORATION

Bread of Life

*To grow in love for Jesus in the
Eucharist and for all humanity.*

Introduction

The Eucharist is Jesus' gift of himself to us. We can recognize his presence physically with us in our particular situation, in our needs, in every aspect of our lives. We begin by adoring Jesus, Divine Master present among us in the Eucharist.

Act of Faith in Jesus' Eucharistic Presence
by Venerable James Alberione

Jesus, eternal Truth, we believe you are really present in the Eucharist. You are here with your body, blood, soul, and divinity. We hear your invitation: "I am the living bread come down from heaven," "Take and eat; this is my body." We believe, O Lord and Master, but increase our faith.

Adoring Jesus Truth

This miraculous story of the feeding of the thousands with just a few loaves and fish is in all four Gospels. It was an important story for the first Christians. As we read it now, we ask the Holy Spirit to be with us and help us discover how this story is important for us.

Reading   John 6:1–15

After this Jesus went off to the other side of the Sea of Galilee of Tiberias. A large crowd was following him because they saw the signs he was performing on the sick. So Jesus went up the mountain and sat down there with his disciples. Now the Passover, the festival of the Jews, was near. When Jesus raised his eyes and saw that a large crowd was coming toward him he said to Philip, "Where can we buy loaves for them to eat?" He said this to test him—he knew what he was going to do. Philip answered him, "Two hundred denarii worth of bread wouldn't be enough to allow each of them to have a little!" One of his disciples, Andrew, Simon Peter's brother, said to him, "There's a boy here who has five barley loaves and two fish, but what are they for so many?" Jesus said, "Have the people sit down"—now there was a lot of grass at that spot. So the men, numbering about five thousand, sat down. Jesus took the loaves and after blessing them he distributed them to those who were reclining, and likewise with the fish, as much as they wanted. When they were full he said to his disciples, "Gather the left-over fragments so nothing will be lost." So they gathered them and filled twelve baskets with fragments of the barley loaves which were left by those who had eaten. When the people saw the sign he'd done they said, "Truly this is the Prophet who is to come into the world!" But when Jesus realized that they intended to come and take him by force to make him king he withdrew alone to the mountain again.

Reflection

Nature gives us hints of how lavishly generous God is: the abundance of strawberries in a strawberry patch, the countless brilliant wildflowers growing in a field. When Jesus miraculously multiplied the bread, there were twelve baskets of fragments left over after the crowd had eaten their fill! Jesus, the very image of God, demonstrates God's generosity with us. Likewise, an abundance of grace awaits us in the Eucharist, the Bread of Life.

God wants to give us an abundance of life and to live in ever deeper communion with us. How do we experience our prayer, our relationship with Jesus in the Eucharist, as life-giving?

Following Jesus Way

Realizing the abundance that Jesus offers us in the Eucharist, our spontaneous response is humble gratitude. In thanksgiving for the gift of the Eucharist, pray slowly the words of a favorite Eucharistic hymn such as "Godhead Here in Hiding," "Gift of Finest Wheat," or the "Holy, holy, holy" from the Eucharistic Celebration.

HOUR
3

Jesus gave us the ultimate example of selflessness and unconditional love. How have we been able to share the love and life that we have received with others? What aspects of our life feel like a struggle, restraining, or lifeless? Take a few moments to speak honestly with Jesus, the one who loves us into life, about the ways that we have not shared God's love with others.

Pause to reflect on the challenges of your life, confronting them with the words and example of Jesus.

We express our sorrow and trust in the Lord.

Act of Hope in Jesus' Eucharistic Presence
by Venerable James Alberione

Jesus, sole Way of salvation, you invite us:
"Learn from me." But we resemble you so little!

Lord, we are not worthy to receive you,
but only say the word and we shall be healed.

Jesus, you pleased the Father; you are our Way.
Draw us to yourself, and give us the grace
to love one another as you have loved us.

Sharing Jesus' Life

Jesus says, "Whoever comes to me will never be hungry, and whoever believes in me will never be thirsty" (John 6:27, 35). What do we hunger for in our everyday life? What are the deeper longings of our hearts, the ones

HOUR
3

we glimpse in times of quiet reflection? Take a few moments to speak to the Lord about the deepest desires of your heart.

Pray the following prayer, *Appeals to Jesus Master,* taking time with each petition, and asking Jesus to transform our hearts to become more Christ-like. We can believe that Jesus really wants to give us these gifts of grace. When we are finished, we can go back and pray the entire prayer again for someone we would like to pray for, substituting his or her name for "me" and "my." At the end, we can add our own personal invocation for that person.

Appeals to Jesus Master
by Venerable James Alberione

Jesus Master, sanctify my mind
     and increase my faith.
Jesus, teaching in the Church,
     draw everyone to yourself.
Jesus Master, deliver me from error,
     empty thoughts and eternal blindness.
Jesus Way between the Father and us,
     I offer you everything and await all from you.
Jesus Way of sanctity, help me imitate you faithfully.
Jesus Way, may I respond wholeheartedly
     to the Father's call to holiness.
Jesus Life, live in me so that I may live in you.
Jesus Life, do not ever permit anything
     to separate me from you.

HOUR
3

Jesus Life, grant that I may live eternally
    in the joy of your love.
Jesus Truth, may you shine in the world through me.
Jesus Way, may I be a faithful mirror
    of your example for others.
Jesus Life, may I be a channel of your grace
    and consolation to others.

Act of Love in Jesus' Eucharistic Presence
by Venerable James Alberione

O Jesus, my Life, our joy and source of all good, we love you. We ask you that we may love you always more, and all those you have redeemed.

You are the vine and we are the branches; we want to remain united to you always so as to bear much fruit.

You are the source: pour out an ever greater abundance of grace to sanctify us.

You are the head and we are your members: communicate to us your Holy Spirit with all the Spirit's gifts.

May your kingdom come through Mary.

Console and save those dear to us. Bring those who have died into your presence. Assist all who share your mission of spreading the Good News. Bless many with vocations to the priesthood and religious life. Amen.

As we conclude our hour of adoration with this act of love, we ask Jesus to help us imitate his selfless love in our daily lives.

HOUR OF ADORATION

Light of the World

*To walk by the light of Christ
and share it with others.*

(Note: If possible, bring a candle you can light before
the Blessed Sacrament.)

Introduction

Take a few deep breaths and try to put aside your distractions, your worries and concerns. Remember that you are in the presence of Jesus in the Eucharist, and that his attention is focused on spending this time with you.

Adoring Jesus Truth

Ask the Holy Spirit to enlighten you as you prepare to read the Word of God.

Sequence to the Holy Spirit

Holy Spirit, Lord of light!
From thy clear celestial height,

Thy pure, beaming radiance give.
Come, thou Father of the poor!
Come, with treasures which endure!
Come, thou light of all that live!
Thou of all consolers best,
Visiting the troubled breast,
Dost refreshing peace bestow;
Thou in toil art comfort sweet,
Pleasant coolness in the heat;
Solace in the midst of woe.
Light immortal! Light divine!
Visit thou these hearts of thine,
And our inmost being fill.
If thou take thy grace away,
Nothing pure in man will stay;
All his good is turned to ill.
Heal our wounds—our strength renew;
On our dryness pour thy dew;
Wash the stains of guilt away.
Bend the stubborn heart and will;
Melt the frozen, warm the chill;
Guide the steps that go astray.
Thou, on those who evermore
Thee confess and thee adore,
In thy sevenfold gifts descend.
Give them comfort when they die;
Give them life with thee on high;
Give them joys which never end. Amen!

John arranges his Gospel so that Jesus' miracles often illustrate a fundamental truth about his identity. What do Jesus' words mean to you?

Reading   John 9:1–40

As he passed along he [Jesus] saw a man who was blind from birth. The disciples asked him, "Rabbi, who sinned, this fellow or his parents, that he should be born blind?" Jesus answered, "Neither he nor his parents sinned—he was born blind so that the works of God might be revealed through him! We must do the works of the One Who sent me while it is day; night is coming, when no one is able to work. As long as I am in the world, I am the light of the world." Having said these things he spit on the ground and made clay out of the spittle, and he smeared the clay on the man's eyes and said to him, "Go wash yourself in the pool of Siloam," which is translated, "Sent." So he went off and washed himself and came back seeing. His neighbors and those who used to see him as a beggar said, "Isn't this the man who used to sit and beg?" Some said, "It is him!" others said, "No, it's not! He only looks like him." The man said, "I'm the one!" So they said to him, "How were your eyes opened?" He answered, "The man called Jesus made clay and smeared it on my eyes and said to me, 'Go to Siloam and wash yourself!' When I went off and washed myself I could see." And they said to him, "Where is he?" He said, "I don't know."

They brought him to the Pharisees—the man who was formerly blind. Now it was the Sabbath on the day that Jesus made the clay and opened his eyes. Once again they as well as the Pharisees asked him how it was that he could see. "He put clay on my eyes," he said, "and I washed myself and now I can see." So some of the Pharisees said, "This man isn't from God because he doesn't keep the Sabbath!" Others said, "How can a sinful man do such signs?" And there was a split among them. So they said to the blind man again, "What do you say about him, since it was your eyes he opened?" Then he said, "He's a prophet."

The Jews didn't believe that the man had been born blind and had gained his sight until they called the parents of the man who was now able to see and asked them, "Is this your son, the one you say was born blind? How can he now see?" His parents answered, "We know that this is our son and that he was born blind, but how he can now see we don't know, nor do we know who opened his eyes. Ask him; he's of age! He can speak for himself!" His parents said these things because they were afraid of the Jews, for the Jews had already agreed that anyone who declared Jesus to be the Messiah would be banished from the synagogue. Therefore, his parents said, "He's of age, ask him!"

So for a second time they summoned the man who had been blind and said to him, "Give glory to God! We know this man's a sinner." He answered, "Whether he's a sinner, I don't know. One thing I do know—I was blind, but now I can see." So they said to him, "What did he do to you? How did he open your eyes?" He answered them, "I've already told you but you didn't listen. Why do you want to hear it again? Surely you don't want to become his disciples, too, do you?" Then they began to insult him and said, "You're his disciple, but we are Moses' disciples! We know that God spoke to Moses, but we don't know where this fellow's from!" The man answered, "The wonder is certainly in this, that you don't know where he's from, yet he opened my eyes. We know God doesn't listen to sinners, but if anyone is God-fearing and does His will He listens to him. It hasn't been heard of from all eternity that someone opened the eyes of a man blind from birth. If this man weren't from God, he wouldn't have been able to do anything." They answered, "You were completely born in sin, and you're teaching us?" And they threw him out.

Jesus heard that they'd thrown him out, and when he found him he said, "Do you believe in the Son of Man?" He answered, "And who is he, Lord, so I can believe in him?" Jesus said to him, "You have seen him, and the one who is speaking with you is he." Then he said, "I believe, Lord," and worshipped him. And Jesus said, "For judgment I came into the world, so that

Those who do not see may see,
And those who see may become blind."

Those of the Pharisees who were with him heard, and they said to him, "We're not blind, too, are we?" Jesus

HOUR
4

said to them, "If you were blind you'd have no sin, but since you say, 'We see!' your sin remains."

Reflection

Jesus uses the powerful images of darkness and light to describe his mission. As metaphors, darkness and light are loaded with symbolic meaning. Think back to a time when you were alone in the dark and had difficulty finding your way. How did it feel to finally find the light?

Everyone has been in a dark place, spiritually as well as physically. Can you remember a difficult time when Jesus' presence or words were a light for you? Jesus wants to cast light on the darkness that makes us afraid. What darkness in your life do you want to bring to Jesus now and ask him to enlighten?

In response to the Scripture reading, write a personal act of faith in Jesus, the light of your life. Your act of faith should reflect the challenges you face in living a Christian life. Or, choose an act of faith you have read in the Gospels or in a prayer book. Such acts of faith can be very short and simple, "My Lord and my God!" or they can be longer, such as the Apostles' Creed. If possible, light a candle and while holding it, pray this act of faith.

Following Jesus Way

God has given us many sources of light: the sun, the full moon on a dark night, the radiance of the Risen Mas-

ter beckoning us on to a future of hope. Let us thank God
for the many ways he gives us light by praying the pro-
logue of the Gospel of John.

In the beginning was the Word,
And the Word was with God,

And the Word was God.
He was in the beginning with God.

All things came to be through him,
And without him nothing came to be.

What came to be through him was life,
And the life was the light of men,

And the light shines in the darkness,
And the darkness did not overcome it.

There was a man sent by God named John. He came as
a witness to bear witness concerning the light, so that all
might believe through him. He was not the light, but came
to bear witness concerning the light. It was the true light
that enlightens every man that was coming into the world.

He was in the world, and the world
        was made by him,
Yet the world did not know him.

He came to his own home,
Yet his own people did not receive him.

But all who did receive him, to them he gave the power
to become sons of God, to those who believe in his name,

HOUR
4

those who were born, not of blood nor of the will of flesh nor of the will of a man, but of God.

And the Word became flesh
And dwelt among us,

And we saw his glory,
Glory as of the only begotten of the Father,

Full of grace and truth.

John bore witness concerning him and cried out, saying, "This was the one of whom I said, 'The one who's coming after me is above me, because he was before me.'"

For we have all received of his fullness,

and grace upon grace,

For the Torah was given through Moses,
Grace and truth came through Jesus Christ.

No one has ever seen God;
The only begotten Son of God,

who is in the bosom of the Father,

he has revealed Him.

John 1:1–18

Jesus said, "You are the light of the world…. Let your light so shine before others that they'll see your good works and glorify your Father in Heaven" (Matthew 5:14, 16). In a dark place, even the smallest light takes on a great importance. To be the light of the world is an awesome call to let the Lord's radiance shine through us to others.

How do you feel that you have reflected the Lord's light to others? Have there been times when you might have blocked light, rather than let God's light shine through you?

Pause to reflect on the challenges you face in your everyday life and to confront them with the words and example of Jesus.

Act of Trust

Jesus Master, Way, Truth and Life,
    have mercy on me.
Jesus Master, save me!
    I want to follow the way of life.
Jesus Master, draw my heart to you!

Sharing Jesus' Life

Let the light of Jesus' love warm your heart. Take some time to pray Psalm 27, basking in the light of God's presence. Ask God to help you understand how you are called to transmit God's light to others in your present situation.

Psalm 27

The LORD is my light and my salvation;
    whom shall I fear?
The LORD is the stronghold of my life;
    of whom shall I be afraid?

When evildoers assail me
    to devour my flesh—

HOUR
4

my adversaries and foes—
    they shall stumble and fall.

Though an army encamp against me,
    my heart shall not fear;
though war rise up against me,
    yet I will be confident.

One thing I asked of the LORD,
    that will I seek after:
to live in the house of the LORD
    all the days of my life,
to behold the beauty of the LORD,
    and to inquire in his temple.

For he will hide me in his shelter
    in the day of trouble;
he will conceal me under the cover of his tent;
    he will set me high on a rock.

Now my head is lifted up
    above my enemies all around me,
and I will offer in his tent
    sacrifices with shouts of joy;
I will sing and make melody to the LORD.

Hear, O LORD, when I cry aloud,
    be gracious to me and answer me!
"Come," my heart says, "seek his face!"
    Your face, LORD, do I seek.
    Do not hide your face from me.

Do not turn your servant away in anger,
    you who have been my help.
Do not cast me off, do not forsake me,
    O God of my salvation!
If my father and mother forsake me,
    the LORD will take me up.

Teach me your way, O LORD,
    and lead me on a level path
    because of my enemies.
Do not give me up to the will of my adversaries,
    for false witnesses have risen against me,
    and they are breathing out violence.

I believe that I shall see the goodness of the LORD
    in the land of the living.
Wait for the LORD;
    be strong, and let your heart take courage;
    wait for the LORD!

*As you conclude this hour of adoration, ask for the grace
to radiate God's love to those you meet today.*

HOUR
4

HOUR OF ADORATION

Disciples in the Footsteps of the Master

To hear and answer the call to serve.

Introduction

Jesus' way of life was one of love—love for the Father and for each person made in God's image. Jesus Master invites you to follow his example of loving service. Spend a few moments in silent adoration of the Master who loves you so much.

Adoring Jesus Truth

Ask the Holy Spirit to set your heart on fire with love, so that its light may help you see in a new way and its heat may melt away your resistance to Jesus' invitation to serve.

Reading   John 13:1–15

Before the festival of the Passover Jesus, knowing that his hour had come to leave this world for the Father, having loved his own in the world, he loved them to the end.

During the banquet, when the Devil had already put it into the heart of Judas son of Simon Iscariot to hand Jesus over, knowing that the Father had given all things into his hands and that he had come from God and was now returning to God, he got up from the banquet and laid aside his cloak, and he took a towel and wrapped it around himself. Then he poured water into the washbasin and began to wash the disciples' feet and wipe them dry with the towel he'd wrapped around himself. When he came to Simon Peter, Peter said to him, "Lord, are you going to wash my feet?" Jesus answered and said to him, "What I'm doing you don't understand just now, but later you'll understand." Peter said to him, "You'll never wash my feet!" Jesus answered him, "Unless I wash you, you will have no share in me." Simon Peter said to him, "Lord, wash not only my feet, but my hands and head as well!" Jesus said to him, "Whoever has bathed has no need to wash except his feet; on the contrary, he's completely purified; and you are pure, but not all of you." For he knew who was to hand him over; that's why he said, "Not all of you are pure."

After he had washed their feet and had put his cloak back on he sat down again and said to them, "Do you understand what I've done for you? You call me 'The Teacher' and 'The Lord,' and rightly so, because I am. So if I, the Lord and Teacher, have washed your feet, you, too, ought to wash each other's feet, because I have given you an example so that, just as I have done for you, you, too, should do."

Reflection

On page 32, there is a beautiful painting by Sieger Koder of Jesus washing the feet of Peter. Jesus is bent over, almost crouched to the floor, and his face is hidden. Peter is leaning over Jesus, familiarly placing one hand on Jesus' shoulder. But Peter's other hand is thrust out as if to push Jesus away in dismay. Did Peter feel unworthy of Jesus' loving gesture? Perhaps Peter felt the same unworthiness that we sometimes feel when we realize we are loved unconditionally. What would you have felt or done in Peter's place? Jesus loves you with the same intensity and proved this love, not by washing your feet, but by dying and rising for love of you.

Act of Faith in Jesus' Love for Us
by Venerable James Alberione

Jesus, Divine Master, we thank and praise your most gentle Heart, which led you to give your life for us. Your blood, your wounds, the scourges, the thorns, the cross, your bowed head—all tell our hearts: "No one loves more than he who gives his life for the loved one." The Shepherd died to give life to the sheep. We too want to spend our lives for you. Grant that always, everywhere, and in all things we may seek to know your will in our lives. Inflame our hearts with a deep love for you and for others.

HOUR
5

Following Jesus Way

Take a few moments to thank Jesus for the many ways he has shown his love for you throughout your life. Make Saint Paul's great hymn to love your thanksgiving.

> Love is patient; love is kind; love is not envious or boastful or arrogant or rude. It does not insist on its own way; it is not irritable or resentful. It does not rejoice in wrongdoing, but rejoices in the truth. It bears all things, believes all things, hopes all things, endures all things. Love never ends.
>
> *1 Corinthians 13:4–8 (NRSV)*

Jesus said, "I have given you an example so that, just as I have done for you, you, too, should do" (John 13:15). Jesus' example of loving service challenges all of us to look into our own lives and evaluate our love in light of his. We are Jesus' hands and feet to serve those in need in our own day. Jesus wants to act through us.

Koder's painting has a detail with profound implications. Although Jesus' face cannot be seen directly, its reflection can be glimpsed in the water in the basin at Peter's feet. Perhaps Koder was trying to share an insight: It is in serving others that we discover the face of Christ.

Pause to reflect on the ways you feel called to serve others in your everyday life and confront how you respond to that call with the words and example of Jesus.

HOUR
5

Express your sorrow to the Lord with the following litany.

For the times I have been impatient,
   Lord, have mercy!
For the times I have been unkind,
   Lord, have mercy!
For the times I have acted jealously,
   Lord, have mercy!

For my prideful boasting, *Lord, have mercy!*
For having acted arrogantly, *Lord, have mercy!*
For having acted dishonestly, *Lord, have mercy!*

For those times when I have acted selfishly,
   Lord, have mercy!
For responding irritably to others,
   Lord, have mercy!
For my brooding over past wrongs,
   Lord, have mercy!

For the times I rejoiced not in truth, but at injustice,
   Lord, have mercy!
For the times when I gave up on others,
   Lord, have mercy!
For my lack of faith and hope, *Lord, have mercy!*
For setting limits to my love, *Lord, have mercy!*

Despite your weaknesses and fears, Jesus invites you, "Come, follow me!" Ask Jesus to show you how he is calling you to serve him more faithfully today, and ask for the grace of self-emptying love:

HOUR
5

Prayer to Imitate Jesus, Divine Servant

Christ Jesus, transform my mind and heart so that I can more faithfully serve you. Give me your own perspective: respect for my dignity as created in the image of God, without pretending that I am equal to God or above others. Empty me of self-importance, and grant me humility—the ability to fully accept the truth about my place in the world.

Form me into your faithful and loving servant. Grant me the ability to recognize when to put others' needs ahead of my own. Bless me with compassion, patience, kindness and perseverance in serving others. May I be attentive and responsive to God's call to serve, even when it is not easy.

When I feel the weight of others' burdens, help me to recognize that you are with me and help me to carry the load. May my love for others be a reflection of your love. I worship you as my Lord and Master, the One who came not to be served, but to serve. Help me to be faithful to your Word: "Love one another as I have loved you."

Sharing Jesus' Life

Jesus' lasting command is to love one another as he has loved us. Reach out in prayer now to others and bring before the Eucharistic Jesus the intentions of the world: the people who struggle with the darkness of pain, violence, war, abuse, disease, selfishness.

Now ask Jesus to transform you into a servant who is attentive to the needs of others and reaches out in love.

Litany of Service
(based on Isaiah 42, 49, 50 and 52)

Lord, I believe that I am your chosen servant whom you uphold. *Send your spirit upon me.* (42:1)

Lord, I believe that you have taken me by the hand and formed me. *Make me a light for those in darkness.* (42:6)

Lord, I believe you called me before I was born and named me. *Make me your faithful servant through whom you will be glorified.* (49:1, 3)

Lord, sometimes I think I have worked in vain and that I have spent my strength for nothing. *Help me remember that you are my strength and my reward is in you.* (49:4).

Lord, each morning you open my ears that I may hear and speak your words: comfort to the weary, encouragement to those who are oppressed. *The Lord God helps me.* (50:4, 5, 7)

Lord, I offer whatever I suffer as a way to share in the hardships suffered by your people. *Give me the peace of surrender to your will and the courage to oppose oppression.* (52)

Add your own petitions to become a more faithful servant.

Pray about one way in which you can go beyond the ordinary scope of your daily life to reach out to those who are suffering.

Concluding Prayer
(based on 2 Corinthians 4)

Lord, I am an earthenware vessel in which you have placed a treasure. Help me to reveal your extraordinary power. When I feel afflicted, free me from constraints. When I am perplexed, lead me beyond despair. When I feel persecuted, do not forsake me. When I am struck down, renew your life in me. As I carry within myself the death of Jesus, may the life of Jesus, too, be revealed in me. Help me to realize that death at work in me means life to those for whom I offer myself. Do not let me lose heart, but grant me abundant grace, so that my thanksgiving may overflow to the glory of God.

Carry in prayer today a particular person or group of people who are suffering.

HOUR
5

Hour of Adoration

Remain in Me

To rejoice in Jesus' presence with us in everyday life.

Introduction

Jesus invites you, "Remain in me." Rejoice that you are in the presence of the Eucharistic Master.

Prayer to the Divine Master
by Venerable James Alberione

Master, You are the Way: I want to walk in Your footsteps and imitate Your example. You are the Truth: enlighten me! You are Life: give me grace!

Adoring Jesus Truth

During the Last Supper, Jesus opened his heart to his disciples. These final words of Jesus spoken during his earthly life have a poignant significance for every follower of Christ.

Reading

John 15:1–17

"I am the true vine,
And my Father is the vinedresser.
Every branch in me that doesn't bear fruit
    He will remove,
And every one bearing fruit He will prune
    so it will bear more fruit.
You are already pure because of the word I have
    spoken to you;
Abide in me, and I will abide in you.
Just as the branch cannot bear fruit on its own
    unless it remains on the vine,
Likewise *you* cannot unless you abide in me.
I am the vine, you are the branches.
Whoever abides in me, and I in him,
He it is who bears much fruit,
For apart from me you can do nothing.
Unless someone abides in me he's thrown out
    like a branch and withers,
And they gather them and throw them into the fire
    and they're burned.
If you abide in me, and my words abide in you,
Ask whatever you wish and it will happen for you.
In this is my Father glorified,
That you bear much fruit and become my disciples.
As the Father loved me, I, too, have loved you;
Abide in my love.

HOUR
6

If you keep my commandments you'll abide
    in my love,
Just as I've kept my Father's commandments
    and I abide in Him."
"I have told you these things so that my joy
    may be in you
and your joy may be complete.
This is my commandment,
    that you love one another as I have loved you.
Greater love than this no man has—
    to lay down his life for his friends.
You are my friends
    if you do what I command you.
I no longer call you servants,
    because the servant doesn't know
      what his lord does.
I have called you friends,
    because everything I have heard from the Father
      I've made known to you.
You have not chosen me;
    on the contrary, I chose you.
And I designated you to go and bear fruit
    and that your fruit should abide,
So that whatever you ask the Father for in my name
    He will give you.
This I command you,
    that you love one another."

HOUR
6

Reflection

In this passage, Jesus asks or encourages you seven times to remain in him. He uses the image of the vine and branches to describe his union with his disciples. How does this image speak to you?

Many mystics have sought to describe their relationship with God through images. In a time of spiritual darkness, Therese of Lisieux described the desolation she felt with the image of a child's ball, eager to be played with but lying forgotten in a corner. Another mystic, Mechtild of Magdeburg, wrote a short poem full of images about her relationship with God:

Lord, You are my lover,
My longing,
My flowing stream,
My sun,
And I am your reflection.

(translated by Oliver Davies)

What image best describes your relationship with Jesus right now? How do you want to respond to Jesus' invitation to you to "remain in him"?

For further reflection, you may wish to write about or sketch this image in your journal or on a blank piece of paper.

Following Jesus Way

The mystery of God's desire to be united with you, manifested definitively by the Incarnation and the Paschal Mystery, inspires awe. Jesus wants to remain intimately connected to you, as a vine is to its branches. The vine that connects you to Jesus is his own life, his love flowing into you.

Just as a branch can become diseased or start to separate from the vine, so every follower of Christ experiences obstacles that prevent Jesus' love from flowing freely in him or her. These impediments often cause great suffering. Overcoming them can be painful, but it is a different kind of pain—a pain that gives growth. Jesus hints at the suffering of a disciple's growth when he talks about pruning the branches and bearing fruit. What in your life needs pruning? How do you feel you have broken away from the vine of God's love? How might you be resisting God's call to grow?

Pause to reflect on the challenges you face in your everyday life and to confront them with the words and example of Jesus.

As we realize how we have let various obstacles prevent us from growing in deeper union with God, we also become aware of God's overwhelming desire to be close to us. Our sorrow becomes a hymn of thanksgiving for God's loving forgiveness and desire to remain in us. Pray Psalm 51 as both a hymn and an expression of your desire to grow closer to God.

Psalm 51

Have mercy on me, O God,
    according to your steadfast love;
according to your abundant mercy
    blot out my transgressions.
Wash me thoroughly from my iniquity,
    and cleanse me from my sin.

For I know my transgressions,
    and my sin is ever before me.
Against you, you alone, have I sinned,
    and done what is evil in your sight,
so that you are justified in your sentence
    and blameless when you pass judgment.
Indeed, I was born guilty,
    a sinner when my mother conceived me.

You desire truth in the inward being;
    therefore teach me wisdom in my secret heart.
Purge me with hyssop, and I shall be clean;
    wash me, and I shall be whiter than snow.
Let me hear joy and gladness;
    let the bones you have crushed rejoice.
Hide your face from my sins,
    and blot out all my iniquities.

Create in me a clean heart, O God,
 and put a new and right spirit within me.
Do not cast me away from your presence,
 and do not take your holy spirit from me.
Restore to me the joy of your salvation,
 and sustain in me a willing spirit.
Then I will teach transgressors your ways,
 and sinners will return to you.
Deliver me from bloodshed, O God,
 O God of my salvation,
 and my tongue will sing aloud of your deliverance.

O Lord, open my lips,
 and my mouth will declare your praise.
For you have no delight in sacrifice;
 if I were to give a burnt offering,
  you would not be pleased.
The sacrifice acceptable to God is a broken spirit;
 a broken and contrite heart, O God,
  you will not despise.

Do good to Zion in your good pleasure;
 rebuild the walls of Jerusalem,
then you will delight in right sacrifices,
 in burnt offerings and whole burnt offerings;
 then bulls will be offered on your altar.

Sharing Jesus' Life

Father James Alberione said, "Like a branch ever bearing fruit and offering it to all, Mary always gives Jesus."

HOUR
6

Mary was able to bring others to her Son Jesus because she was the person who most closely lived in union with him. Mary was the first to welcome Jesus into her life, and she was the first to present Jesus to others—to her cousin Elizabeth, to the shepherds, to the Magi, and throughout her life.

Mary's life of union with Jesus encourages us to draw close to the vine of God's love. Pray the Joyful Mysteries of the Rosary, attentive to the moments of union that Mary experienced with Jesus during their ordinary life together. Ask Mary to help you to draw closer to Jesus in your own every day life.

Pray the Joyful Mysteries of the Rosary (see page 183).

As you conclude your hour of adoration with an act of love for the God who desires to be so close to you, choose one way you can share God's love with someone who is in need, perhaps someone in your family.

HOUR OF ADORATION

Mary, Faithful Disciple of the Master

*To follow Jesus Master in the company of Mary,
the first disciple and a woman of the Word.*

Introduction

Mary was the first and most faithful disciple of Jesus, a firsthand witness of Jesus' private life, and always his close follower, even when he was dying on the cross. Mary's presence gives us strength and support in following Jesus.

Adoring Jesus Truth

As we read this familiar passage about the Incarnation, we reflect especially on Mary's response of faith.

Reading

Luke 1:26–38

Now in the sixth month the angel Gabriel was sent from God to a city of Galilee named Nazareth, to a virgin who was betrothed to a man of the house of David named

Joseph, and the virgin's name was Mary. And when he came into her presence he said, "Hail, full of grace, the Lord is with you!" She was perplexed by these words and wondered what sort of greeting this could be. Then the angel said to her,

> "Fear not, Mary—
>> you have found grace before the Lord.
> And, behold, you will conceive in your womb
>> and will bear a son,
>> and you shall name him Jesus.
> He will be great and will be called
>> Son of the Most High,
>>> and the Lord God will give him the throne
>>> of his father, David.
> He will reign over the house of Jacob forever,
>> and his Kingdom will have no end."

Mary said to the angel, "How will this come about, since I do not know man?" And in answer the angel said to her,

> "The Holy Spirit will come upon you,
> And the power of the Most High
>> will overshadow you;
> Therefore the holy child to be born
>> will be called the Son of God.

> And, behold, your kinswoman Elizabeth, even she
>> conceived a son in her old age,

HOUR
7

And this is the sixth month for her who was
    called barren.

For **nothing will be impossible for God."**

And Mary said,

"Behold, the handmaid of the Lord;
    let it be done to me according to your word."

Then the angel went away from her.

Reflection

Because we have heard or read this passage so often,
we can forget that for Mary, the annunciation must have
been startling, even disturbing. In one moment, Mary received a call that, if accepted, would forever change her
life and upset all her plans. Yet, Mary believed in God's
faithful love and put her trust unequivocally in the God
who called her in such an unexpected way.

There is a call from God for us in every situation.
Maybe the call does not seem to be for anything that is
important, but it is an invitation nonetheless. For example,
in a split second, we decide which service is more important at that moment: to stop to talk to someone or to focus
on the task awaiting us. God speaks to us in our everyday
situations. Silence and a listening heart enable us to hear
God's calls, both great and small. How often are we able
to listen for God's invitation, and when we hear it, how do
we respond?

HOUR
7

Prayer after Reading Sacred Scripture
by Venerable James Alberione

Jesus, Divine Master,
you have words of eternal life.
We believe, O Lord and Truth,
but increase our faith.
We love you, O Lord and Way, with all our strength.
We pray to you, O Lord and Life.
We adore you, praise you,
beseech you, and thank you
for the gift of Sacred Scripture.
With Mary, we shall remember
and preserve your words in our minds
and we shall contemplate them in our hearts.
Jesus Master, Way and Truth and Life,
have mercy on us.

Following Jesus Way

John Paul II tells us, "The Blessed Virgin…becomes a model for those who accept Christ's words. Believing in the divine message since the annunciation and fully supporting the Person of the Son, she teaches us to listen to the Savior with trust, to discover in him the divine Word who transforms and renews our life."[15]

We believe that the Word of God can change us. Take a few minutes to reflect on how God's Word has made a difference in your life. Perhaps a favorite Scripture pas-

HOUR
7

sage has given you great encouragement in a moment of darkness. After pondering the power of God's Word in your own life, pray Mary's beautiful hymn of thanksgiving, the Magnificat (p. 40–41).

Now pause to reflect on the challenges you face in your everyday life, confronting them with the words and example of Jesus. Use these questions as a guide:

How often do you meditate on the Word of God? How aware are you of God's saving action in your own personal life? How have you prayed for guidance in situations you struggle with? What invitations from God have you ignored lately?

After making a personal act of contrition, pray these verses of Psalm 119, deciding how you can give the Word of God more importance in your life.

Psalm 119:10 – 16, 105

With my whole heart I seek you;
    do not let me stray from your commandments.
I treasure your word in my heart,
    so that I may not sin against you.
Blessed are you, O LORD;
    teach me your statutes.
With my lips I declare
    all the ordinances of your mouth.
I delight in the way of your decrees
    as much as in all riches.

HOUR
7

I will meditate on your precepts,
    and fix my eyes on your ways.
I will delight in your statutes;
    I will not forget your word.

Your word is a lamp to my feet
    and a light to my path.

Sharing Jesus' Life

In the following prayer, we ask Mary to pray that we live fully the gift of faith—a faith that is attuned to God's call and transforms our lives.

Prayer to our Lady of the Annunciation
by Venerable James Alberione

May all generations proclaim you blessed, Mary.

You believed the Archangel Gabriel,
and in you were fulfilled all the great things
that were announced to you.

My soul and my entire being praise you, Mary.

You believed completely in the incarnation
of the Son of God in your virginal womb,
and you became the Mother of God.

Then the happiest day in the history of the world
dawned. Humanity received the Divine Master,
the sole eternal Priest, the One who would die
to save us, the universal King.

Faith is a gift of God and the root of holiness.
Mary, obtain for us, too, a lively, firm and active
faith—a faith which enables us to accept salvation
and the gift of holiness. Obtain for us faith in the
Church, in the Gospel, in eternal life.

May we meditate on the words of your blessed Son,
as you preserved them in your heart and devoutly
meditated on them.

May the Gospel be preached to everyone.

May it be eagerly accepted.

May all people become, in Jesus Christ,
children of God. Amen.

A popular title given to Mary in the early Church is
Queen of Apostles. Because she cooperated with God in
bringing Jesus into the world, Mary is honored as both
mother and guide of those who help others to come to
know and love her Son. We entrust all the intentions in
our hearts to Mary's intercession.

Make a mental list of all the people you have had contact with over the past week, and place their intentions,
too, before Mary. Then, ask Mary to help us to recognize
our call to be apostles to the people we live with, work
with and meet every day. Choose a mystery of the Rosary
and pray one decade for these intentions, concluding with
the following prayer to the Queen of Apostles.

Prayer to the Queen of Apostles
by Venerable Thecla Merlo[16]

Queen of Apostles, pray for us!

Pray for us, your children, who entrust ourselves to you. Pray for us so that we may never sin, but may love Jesus with all our hearts.

Beneath your mantle, O Mother, we your children take refuge daily. Gaze on us as a mother; watch over us as your children. All that we are and have we offer to Jesus through you.

Teach us, guide us, sustain us, defend us from every danger as you have done till now. And after this exile, show us Jesus, the blessed fruit of your womb.

As we conclude our hour of adoration, we ask Mary to help us hear God's call to us in our daily life.

HOUR OF  ADORATION

Sacred Heart of the Master

To trust in the love of Christ.

Introduction

Saint Paul powerfully expresses what Christ's love means to him in his letter to the Romans. Paul faced tremendous obstacles in the preaching of the Gospel and gave the ultimate witness to Christ by his martyrdom. It was his relationship with Christ that gave Paul the security to risk everything for the sake of the Gospel.

Adoring Jesus Truth

This rich reading reveals the depth of a true relationship and complete dependence on Christ.

Reading   Ephesians 1:3–23 (NRSV)

Blessed be the God and Father of our Lord Jesus Christ, who has blessed us in Christ with every spiritual blessing in the heavenly places, just as he chose us in Christ before the foundation of the world to be holy and blameless before him in love. He destined us for adoption as his children through Jesus Christ, according to the good pleasure of his will, to the praise of his glorious grace that he freely bestowed on us in the Beloved. In him we have redemption through his blood, the forgiveness of our trespasses, according to the riches of his grace that he lavished on us. With all wisdom and insight he has made known to us the mystery of his will, according to his good pleasure that he set forth in Christ, as a plan for the fullness of time, to gather up all things in him, things in heaven and things on earth. In Christ we have also obtained an inheritance, having been destined according to the purpose of him who accomplishes all things according to his counsel and will, so that we, who were the first to set our hope on Christ, might live for the praise of his glory. In him you also, when you had heard the word of truth, the gospel of your salvation, and had believed in him, were marked with the seal of the promised Holy Spirit; this is the pledge of our inheritance toward redemption as God's own people, to the praise of his glory.

I have heard of your faith in the Lord Jesus and your love toward all the saints, and for this reason I do not cease to give thanks for you as I remember you in my prayers. I pray that the God of our Lord Jesus Christ, the Father of glory, may give you a spirit of wisdom and revelation as you come to know him, so that, with the eyes of your heart enlightened, you may know what is the hope to which he

has called you, what are the riches of his glorious inheritance among the saints, and what is the immeasurable great-
ness of his power for us who believe, according to the
working of his great power. God put this power to work in
Christ when he raised him from the dead and seated him
at his right hand in the heavenly places, far above all rule
and authority and power and dominion, and above every
name that is named, not only in this age but also in the age
to come. And he has put all things under his feet and has
made him the head over all things for the church, which is
his body, the fullness of him who fills all in all.

Reflection

Christ reveals his love for us in innumerable ways:
creating us, blessing us with every spiritual blessing,
choosing us in love to be holy, embracing us as his broth-
ers and sisters, redeeming us, promising us eternal life….
What is the most powerful way that we have experienced
Christ working in our lives? Is there a phrase in this reading which helps us to realize in a fresh way God's overwhelming love for us?

Following Jesus Way

Aware of God's action in our lives, we can pray our
own personal Magnificat in praise of God's goodness to
us. We can begin with the actual words of Mary's prayer,
but then use our own words to praise God for the specific
ways he has worked in our lives.

HOUR
8

As graced as we are, we know that we do not trust enough in the Lord's goodness and love for us. Learning to trust in God is a lifelong journey. Read the following passage and use it to reflect on the ways God is calling us to trust right now:

While he [Jesus] was still speaking some people came from the ruler of the synagogue's household and said, "Your daughter has died; why trouble the teacher further?" But Jesus paid no attention to what was being said and told the ruler of the synagogue, "Do not be afraid; just believe!" And he didn't allow anyone to accompany him except Peter and James and James' brother John. When they came to the leader of the synagogue's house Jesus saw the confusion and the people weeping and wailing loudly, and when he entered he said to them, "Why are you upset and weeping? The child hasn't died, she's sleeping!" And they just laughed at him. But after driving them all out he took the father of the child and the mother and those who were with him, and he went in to where the child was; and after taking hold of the child's hand he said to her, "Talitha koum," which, translated, is, "Little girl, I say to you, arise!" At once the little girl got up and began to walk around—she was twelve years old. And at once they were completely overcome with amazement. Then he gave strict orders that no one should know of this and said to give her something to eat."

Mark 5:35–43

What are your deepest fears? How do they prevent you from acting out of love? How would a greater trust in the Lord change your life?

We pause to reflect on the challenges we face in our everyday lives, especially our fears, and confront them with the words and example of Jesus.

Pray this prayer adapted from Paul's Letter to the Romans as an act of trust in God's tremendous love for you.

If God is for us, who can be against us?
If God didn't spare his own Son but instead gave
    him up for all of us, won't he also freely give us
    everything along with his Son?
Who will accuse God's chosen ones?
    God himself pardons them!
Who will condemn them? Christ died and rose for us
    and is now at God's right hand interceding for us!
Who will separate us from Christ's love?
Affliction, distress, persecution, famine, destitution,
    danger, or the sword?

[Add your own fears here—be as specific as you can.]

In all these things we are winning an overwhelming victory through the One Who loved us.

HOUR
8

We are convinced that neither death nor life, neither angels nor principalities, neither things present nor to come nor powers, neither height nor depth nor any other created being will be able to separate us from God's love in Christ Jesus our Lord.

based on Romans 8:32–39

Sharing Jesus' Life

The following prayer, *Creed of the Called,* is based on the Pauline letters and focuses on the relationship between the disciple and the Father—how we trust God will work in and through our lives.

Creed of the Called

We believe that God chose us in him before the world began, to be holy and blameless in his sight (Ephesians 1:4).

We believe that those whom he foreknew he predestined to share the image of his Son (Romans 8:29).

We believe that God who had set us apart before we were born and called us by his favor chose to reveal his Son to us, that we might spread among all people the good tidings concerning him (Galatians 1:15–16).

We believe that God has saved us and has called us to a holy life, not because of any merit of ours but according to his own design—the grace held out to

us in Christ Jesus before the world began
(2 Timothy 1:12).

We believe that Christ Jesus has judged us faithful
and worthy by calling us to his service
(cf. 1 Timothy 1:12).

We believe that we are apostles by vocation, servants
of Christ Jesus, set apart to announce the Gospel of
God (cf. Romans 1:1).

Considering our vocation, we believe that God chose
the weak of this world to shame the strong, so that
our faith would not rest on the wisdom of men but
on the power of God (cf. 1 Corinthians 1:27; 2:5).

We believe that to each one God has given the
manifestation of the Spirit for the common good
(cf. 1 Corinthians 12:7).

We believe that we must live a life worthy of the
calling which we have received: with perfect humility, meekness and patience, seeking to grow in all
things toward him (cf. Ephesians 4:1–2).

We believe that all things work together for the good
of those who love God, who have been called
according to his decree (cf. Romans 8:28).

We believe in him whose power now at work in us
can do immeasurably more than we ask or imagine
(cf. Ephesians 3:20).

We believe that he who has begun the good work in us will carry it through to completion, right up to the day of Christ Jesus, because he who calls us is Faithful (cf. Philippians 1:6, 1 Thessalonians 5:24).

Convinced that God loves us unconditionally and is always with us, we resolve to take one risk today to more faithfully live out the demands of the Gospel.

HOUR OF ADORATION

With Jesus Crucified

To contemplate the mystery of the crucified Jesus.

(Note: For this hour of adoration, bring with you a copy of the Stations of the Cross. Try to have within sight an image of Jesus' passion—either a crucifix in the church or a holy card with the crucifixion scene.)

Introduction

It is difficult to approach the crucifixion of the Lord. Even the Gospels are terse, stripped of emotion—because when expressing such a great mystery of love, words seem inadequate. Yet the Church has the opportunity to join with Jesus as he renews his supreme sacrifice of love for us in the Eucharistic Celebration every day.

Adoring Jesus Truth

To ponder the mystery of Jesus' suffering and death, read the Gospel of John's story of the crucifixion.

Reading   John 19:16–30

Then he [Pilate] handed him over to them to be crucified.

So they took Jesus in charge. And carrying the cross himself he went out to what was called "the Place of the Skull," in Hebrew, Golgotha, where they crucified him and with him two others, on either side, while Jesus was in the middle. Now Pilate wrote a notice and placed it on the cross, but it was written, "Jesus of Nazareth, the King of the Jews." Many of the Jews read this notice, because the place where Jesus was crucified was near the city, and it was written in Hebrew, Latin, and Greek. So the chief priests of the Jews said to Pilate, "Don't write, 'The King of the Jews' but, 'He said, I am the King of the Jews.'" Pilate answered, "What I have written I have written!"

When the soldiers had crucified Jesus they took his clothes and made four parts, one for each soldier, plus the tunic. Now the tunic was seamless, woven from the top in one piece. So they said to each other, "Let's not tear it; let's draw lots for it instead," so the Scripture would be fulfilled which said,

They divided my garments among them,
and for my clothing they cast lots.

So the soldiers did these things. Now standing by Jesus' cross were his mother and his mother's sister, Mary the wife of Clopas, and Mary Magdalen. When Jesus saw his mother and the disciple he loved standing by he said to his mother, "Woman, here is your son." Then he said to

HOUR
9

the disciple, "Here is your mother." And from that hour the disciple took her into his home.

After this Jesus, knowing that everything had already been accomplished, in order to fulfill the Scripture, said, "I'm thirsty." There was a container there full of sour wine; so after putting a sponge full of sour wine on some hyssop they held it up to his mouth. When he had taken the sour wine Jesus said, "All has been fulfilled!" and bowing his head he gave up the spirit.

Reflection

What impressed you in this reading? What feelings does it stir up in you? Do you believe that Jesus' death 2000 years ago was for you, individually? What do you wish you could have told Jesus that first Good Friday? Take a few moments to study a crucifix or an image of Jesus' passion. Imagine yourself beneath the cross. Focus your attention on Jesus. Speak to him. If no words come, just stay with him in his suffering.

Following Jesus Way

No one is worthy of God's tremendous love. Yet, the reality remains that God does love you. In gratitude, thank God for all the ways God has shown love for you, in both the good times and the bad times.

As an act of thanksgiving, pray the Gloria from the Eucharistic Celebration.

HOUR
9

Knowing that you have been loved so deeply by Jesus, how do you want to love Jesus in return? The most concrete way to show your love for Jesus is to love him in someone near you. Right before his death, Jesus gave a new commandment: "Love one another as I have loved you" (John 15:12). How is Jesus calling you to "lay down" your life (your preferences, your time, your possessions) for others today? What holds you back from loving selflessly?

Pause to reflect on the challenges of your own life, confronting them with the words and example of Jesus.

Express your sorrow for the times you have failed to love, by praying:

Heart of Jesus, Son of the eternal Father,
    have mercy on us.
Heart of Jesus, broken for our sins,
    have mercy on us.
Heart of Jesus, our peace and reconciliation,
    have mercy on us.

Sharing Jesus' Life

To deepen your understanding of how much Jesus has loved you, you can pray the Stations of the Cross. There are many versions of the Stations of the Cross available. Or, choose one scene from Jesus' passion that has always

HOUR
9

stood out for you and imagine yourself there; simply be there with Jesus, and speak to him from your heart.

You may wish to conclude the stations with this beautiful traditional prayer, asking Jesus to help you to bring his love to others throughout the day:

Soul of Christ, sanctify me.
Body of Christ, save me.
Blood of Christ, let me drink your wine
Water flowing from the side of Christ, wash me.
Passion of Christ, strengthen me.
Good Jesus, hear me.
Within thy wounds, hide me
and keep me close to thee.
From the evil enemy defend me.
In the hour of my death, call me
and bid me come to thee,
that with thy saints I may praise thee
through all eternity.

As you conclude your prayer, choose one way you can reach out to someone who is in need.

HOUR
9

HOUR OF ADORATION 10

That You May Have Life

To deepen our life in God.

Introduction

Every person thirsts for fulfillment in life. A deep relationship with Jesus becomes the source of deepest personal fulfillment, giving joy and purpose to every aspect of life.

Adoring Jesus Truth

This intimate story of Jesus and the Samaritan woman is one of the most fascinating dialogues in the Gospels. How does Jesus respond to the woman's bold challenges, her defensiveness, and her simplicity?

Reading   John 4:6–30

Now he had to pass through Samaria, and he came to a Samaritan city named Sychar, near the field Jacob gave to his son Joseph. Now Jacob's well was there. So Jesus, tired out from the journey, simply sat down at the well. It was about noon.

A Samaritan woman came to draw water. Jesus said to her, "Give me a drink"—his disciples had gone off to the city to buy food. So the Samaritan woman said, "How is it that you, a Jew, ask me, a Samaritan woman, for a drink?"—Jews don't use vessels in common with Samaritans. Jesus answered and said to her, "If you knew the gift of God and who it is who's saying to you, 'Give me a drink,' you would have asked him and he would have given you living water." The woman said to him, "Lord, you have no bucket and the well is deep, so where do you get the living water from? Surely you are not greater than our father Jacob who gave us the well and drank from it himself, as well as his sons and his herds?" Jesus answered and said to her, "Everyone who drinks this water will thirst again. But whoever drinks the water I will give him will never thirst; instead, the water I will give him will become a spring of water welling up in him to eternal life." The woman said to him, "Lord, give me this water so I'll neither be thirsty nor have to come over here to draw water."

He said to her, "Go call your husband and come here." The woman answered and said to him, "I don't have a husband." Jesus said to her. "You said well, 'I don't have a husband'—you've had five men and the one you have now isn't your husband. You've spoken the truth." The woman said to him, "Lord, I see that you're a prophet. Our fathers worshipped on this mountain but you say that

Jerusalem is the Place where we should worship." Jesus said to her, "Believe me, woman, the hour is coming when you'll worship the Father neither on this mountain nor in Jerusalem. You worship what you don't know; we worship what we know, because salvation is from the Jews. But the hour is coming, and is now, when the true worshippers will worship the Father in spirit and truth, for the Father also seeks such people who worship Him. God is spirit, and those who worship Him must worship in spirit and truth." The woman said to him, "I know that the Messiah is coming, who is called the Anointed; when he comes he'll tell us everything." Jesus said to her, "I who am speaking to you am he."

At this point his disciples came, and they were amazed that he was speaking to a woman. Nevertheless, no one said, "What do you want?" or, "Why are you speaking with her?" So the woman left her water jar and went off to the city and said to the men, "Come see a man who told me everything I've done! Could this be the Messiah?" They went out of the city and came to him.

Reflection

In this reading, Jesus reveals himself as the gentle Master. His compassionate gaze pierces the defenses of the Samaritan woman, who opens her heart to him. Despite her arguments, Jesus recognizes that she is searching for God. His response is to offer her the way to life.

HOUR
10

In Baptism, each of us received the tremendous gift of sharing in the very life of God, of journeying with Jesus sacramentally through his passion, death, and resurrection. When you were baptized, you or your sponsor promised that you would reject Satan, all his works and empty promises. You affirmed your belief in God the Father; the Son incarnate, Jesus Christ; the Holy Spirit; the Catholic Church; the communion of saints; the forgiveness of sins; the resurrection of the body and everlasting life.

As an act of celebration and recommitment, renew your baptismal promises in your own words.

Following Jesus Way

Jesus Master offers you his very own life in the sacraments, especially in the Eucharistic Celebration. In thanksgiving for the gift of the Eucharist and for all the ways Jesus invites you to life in him, pray:

The Divine Praises

Blessed be God.
Blessed be his Holy Name.
Blessed be Jesus Christ, true God and true Man.
Blessed be the name of Jesus.
Blessed be his most Sacred Heart.
Blessed be his most Precious Blood.
Blessed be Jesus in the most holy Sacrament
    of the Altar.

HOUR
10

Blessed be the Holy Spirit the Paraclete.
Blessed be the great Mother of God,
     Mary most holy.
Blessed be her holy and Immaculate Conception.
Blessed be her glorious Assumption.
Blessed be the name of Mary, Virgin and Mother.
Blessed be Saint Joseph, her most chaste spouse.
Blessed be God in his angels and in his saints.

How sensitively Jesus brought the confused, down-trodden Samaritan woman to express her spiritual longings: "Lord, give me this water..." What are your deepest longings? What are your dreams? Sometimes dreams are meant to be followed. Often, they contain a seed of truth about what is lacking in our lives. What prevents you from following your dreams? Bring these desires to Jesus, and talk with him about them now.

Pause to reflect on your deepest desires and confront them with the words and example of Jesus.

Jesus wants to give us the fullness of life. Pray a personal act of sorrow and trust for not responding to his invitations.

Sharing Jesus' Life

In her dialogue with Jesus, the Samaritan woman initially tried to hide her hurt and deep longings. But when she opened up to Jesus, he responded to both her pain and her yearning.

HOUR
10

Imagine yourself meeting Jesus unexpectedly, when you are doing some ordinary chore. What desires stir in your heart as you see him there, ready to speak to you? What do you want to say to Jesus? And what does Jesus want to say to you? Is there an area or situation in your life that you tend to leave out of your prayer? Can you talk to Jesus about that now?

After some time of personal prayer, make the following prayer your own, adding your own petitions.

Petitions to Jesus Master

Jesus Truth, sanctify my mind, increase my faith. Make sacred all my mental activities: fantasy, imagination, analyzing, judging. Guide me to an ever better and honest knowledge of myself. How much you love and cherish me! I want to recognize your image in me and in all whom I meet today. Let me be gentle—both with myself and with others. Free me from excessive negativity; help me to discover and respond to your call in every situation. Let me not be so caught up in my own plans that I ignore your call.

Jesus Truth, reveal yourself to me. Let me see my life and the world through your eyes. You are present and active in the world today. How do you want to work through me? Let me be preoccupied with the needs of others rather than my own. Jesus Truth, set me free!

Jesus Way, sanctify my will, increase my hope. May all my actions be those of a faithful disciple. I want to focus not on how much I am doing, but on how I am doing it. Teach me to live in the present moment, to be truly aware of where I am and what I am doing. Make me aware of my compulsions and help me learn self-control. Free me from addictive behavior, so that I can direct all my energies to serving you.

Jesus Way, I offer you whatever I do today whole-heartedly for love of you, without worrying about the past or the future. Lead me to trust ever more deeply in your love for me and for every person. May I be fully present to everyone I speak to today, acting with genuine kindness, honesty, and gentle-ness. Make me an instrument of your grace and love in the world.

Jesus Life, sanctify my heart, increase my love for you and for others. In all whom I meet today, may I see an aspect of your divine face. Make me your compassionate and loving disciple. Give me the strength, the enthusiasm, and the joy to persevere in loving service. May your love for every person radiate through me!

My Jesus, my Life, you are the ultimate source of joy, life, and meaning! Draw me so closely to you that our hearts beat with the same desires, the same love, the same life. Make all my life holy, directed to-wards you and lived in you. May I speak the words

HOUR
10

you would speak, do the things that you would do, choose to help those whom no one wants to help. Let me become your loving presence for all whose lives intersect with mine today, however briefly. Jesus Life, teach me how to love as you love. Amen.

Think of some ways you could celebrate the anniversary of your Baptism. Look up the date of your baptism and mark its anniversary on your calendar so that you remember to celebrate the beginning of your covenantal relationship with God.

Hour of Adoration 11

I Am with You

*To share a particular sorrow or
difficulty with the Lord.*

Introduction

This hour of adoration is meant to be used in time of difficulty or sorrow. Open your heart to God and ask God to be with you at this difficult time. Spend a few moments in silent adoration. Ask for the light of the Holy Spirit so that you may feel God's presence and receive comfort.

If during this prayer time you do not feel the presence of the Lord with you, don't be disturbed. Feeling that God is far away is a common experience, especially in times of suffering. Psalm 34 reminds us that God is near to the brokenhearted. If no words come to you during this time of prayer, just try to remember that you are in God's loving presence. That in itself is a powerful prayer of faith.

Adoring Jesus Truth

In this reading, Jesus raises Lazarus from the dead. But first, he weeps with Martha and Mary over the loss of their brother. How is God with you in this time of difficulty? Is God weeping with you? Catching your tears? Embracing you?

Reading   John 11:1–44

Now a certain man was sick, Lazarus of Bethany, from the village of Mary and her sister Martha. Mary was the one who had anointed the Lord with oil and wiped his feet dry with her hair—it was her brother Lazarus who was sick. So the sisters sent to tell him, "Lord, behold, the one you love is sick." When Jesus heard this he said, "This sickness will not bring death—it is for the glory of God so the Son of Man may be glorified through it." Now Jesus loved Martha and her sister and Lazarus, but after he heard that Lazarus was sick he stayed where he was for two more days. Then after this he said to the disciples, "Let's go into Judea again." The disciples said to him, "Rabbi, the Jews were just trying to stone you, and now you're going back there again?" Jesus answered, "Aren't there twelve hours in a day?

If someone walks in the day he doesn't stumble,
    because he sees the light of this world,
But if someone walks in the night he stumbles,
    because the light isn't with him."

HOUR
11

He said these things, and then he said to them, "Our friend Lazarus has fallen asleep, but I'm going now to wake him up." So the disciples said to him, "Lord, if he's fallen asleep he'll recover." But Jesus had spoken about his death, while they thought he was speaking about natural sleep. So then Jesus said to them openly, "Lazarus has died, and I rejoice for your sake that I wasn't there, so you may believe. But let's go to him" So Thomas, who was called the Twin, said to his fellow disciples, "Let's go, too, to die with him!"

When Jesus came he found that Lazarus had already been in the tomb for four days. Now Bethany was near Jerusalem, about two miles away, and many of the Jews had come to Martha and Mary to console them over their brother. So Martha, when she heard that Jesus was coming, met him, but Mary stayed in the house. Martha said to Jesus, "Lord, if you had been here my brother wouldn't have died! but even now I know that whatever you ask God for, God will give you." Jesus said to her, "Your brother will rise!" Martha said to him, "I know that he'll rise at the resurrection on the last day." Jesus said to her,

"*I* am the resurrection and the life!
Whoever believes in me, even if he should die,
    will live,
And everyone who lives and believes in me
    shall never die!

Do you believe this?" She said to him, "Yes, Lord, I've come to believe that you're the Messiah, the Son of God who has come into the world!"

After she said these things she went off and called her sister Mary, saying quietly, "The Teacher is here and he's asking for you." When she heard that, she got up quickly and went to him. Now Jesus had not yet come to the village, but was still at the place where Martha had met him. So the Jews who were with her in the house, consoling her, when they saw that Mary had quickly gotten up and gone out they followed her, thinking, "She's going to the tomb to weep there." When Mary came to where Jesus was and saw him she fell at his feet and said to him, "Lord, if you'd been here my brother wouldn't have died!" So when Jesus saw her weeping, and the Jews who had come with her weeping, he groaned in spirit and was troubled and he said, "Where have you laid him?" They said to him, "Lord, come and see!" Jesus began to weep. So the Jews said, "See how he loved him!" But some of them said, "Couldn't the one who opened the eyes of the blind man have caused this man not to die?"

So Jesus, again groaning within himself, came to the tomb. Now it was a cave, and a stone lay on it. Jesus said, "Take the stone away!" Martha, the sister of the dead man, said to him, "Lord, by now he'll smell—it's been four days!" Jesus said to her, "Didn't I tell you that if you believe you'll see the glory of God?" So they took the stone away. Then Jesus lifted up his eyes and said, "Father, I give you thanks, because You heard me. Now I knew that You always hear me, but I said this for the sake of the crowd standing around me, so they may believe that You sent me." And after saying this he called out with a loud voice, "Lazarus, come out!" The dead man came out with his hands and feet bound with thongs and his face wrapped with a cloth. Jesus said to them, "Untie him and let him go!"

Reflection

As Jesus arrives to console Martha and Mary, and to raise their brother Lazarus from the dead, Martha runs to her sister Mary and tells her, "The Master is here and wants to see you." What powerful words these must have been to the grieving Mary. These words are addressed to you, too. Jesus Master wants to meet you here, where you are. He wants you to sit with him and share your shattered hopes and dreams, your fears and your pain.

After some quiet reflection, pray the following act of faith as a response to the reading.

An Act of Faith in the Lord's Presence

Lord, I believe you are here with me right now, loving me.

But it's dark and I cannot see your radiance.
It's quiet and I cannot hear the tender whisper of your voice. My heart is so broken and afraid that I cannot feel the warmth of your gentle presence.

HOUR
11

I can only pray: Be with me, Lord.
I want to see your face.
I want to know that you are with me.
I want to be cradled in your arms.
I want to feel your strength, your peace.

Even if I can't feel you, hold me tight.
Even if I can't see you, stay right beside me.
Even in the darkest hour, be with me, Lord.

You are the Divine Master: help me
    to discover your presence in every situation.
You walked the way of suffering
    during your earthly life: now walk with me.
You are the Resurrection and the Life, overcoming
    sin and death: fill me with your grace and love.

I cling to your promise: "Do not be afraid, for I am
with you always, until the very end of time." I
entrust myself completely to your merciful love.

Following Jesus Way

The night before Jesus died, he went to pray in the Garden of Gethsemane, and he asked his three disciples, Peter, James, and John, to watch and pray with him. They fell asleep, and Jesus was left all alone in the night. Ask Jesus now to "watch and pray" with you as you face this difficult situation. Ask him not to leave you alone, but to help you discover his presence in your suffering. Listen to Jesus' voice, calling you to grow or respond in this situation.

As you confront your life in light of Jesus' words and example, choose to focus not on your weakness, but on God's presence and love for you.

Renew your trust in the Lord by holding in your mind or repeating aloud a phrase that reminds you that God is with you, such as "God is near to the brokenhearted."

Sharing Jesus' Life

At difficult times, one of the best ways to pray is to pour out your heart to the Lord, telling God your deepest feelings—anger, discouragement, fear, hope, your desires.

The psalms are wonderful, honest prayers of the heart. After you have talked heart-to-heart with the Lord, pray Psalm 42 and make it your heart's cry to the God who loves you.

Psalm 42

As a deer longs for flowing streams
    so my soul longs for you, O God.
My soul thirsts for God,
    for the living God.
When shall I come and behold
    the face of God?
My tears have been my food
    day and night,
while people say to me continually,
    "Where is your God?"

HOUR
11

These things I remember,
　　as I pour out my soul:
how I went with the throng,
　　and led them in procession to the house of God,
with glad shouts and songs of thanksgiving,
　　a multitude keeping festival.
Why are you cast down, O my soul,
　　and why are you disquieted within me?
Hope in God; for I shall again praise him,
　　my help and my God.

My soul is cast down within me;
　　therefore I remember you
from the land of Jordan and of Hermon,
　　from Mount Mizar.
Deep calls to deep
　　at the thunder of your cataracts;
all your waves and your billows
　　have gone over me.
By day the LORD commands his steadfast love,
　　and at night his song is with me,
a prayer to the God of my life.

I say to God, my rock,
　　"Why have you forgotten me?
Why must I walk about mournfully
　　because the enemy oppresses me?"

As with a deadly wound in my body,
    my adversaries taunt me,
while they say to me continually,
    "Where is your God?"

Why are you cast down, O my soul,
    and why are you disquieted within me?
Hope in God; for I shall again praise him,
    my help and my God.

Throughout your day, remember that God is with you.

HOUR
11

HOUR OF ADORATION

Celebrating Our Life in Christ

To praise and share our joy with God.

Introduction

Often, we do not give enough importance to praise and thanksgiving in our prayer. This hour is a celebration—praising God for the many blessings he has given us and sharing our joy with the One who cares the most for our well-being.

We may want to begin this hour of adoration by praying or singing a favorite hymn. Music or singing should be used throughout this hour as much as possible, to express a joyful spirit of praise.

Adoring Jesus Truth

The Pauline letters point out to us many reasons for immense joy and gratitude. Thanksgiving is an integral part of a relationship with Christ and through Christ, with the Father.

Readings   1 Thessalonians 5:16 – 24 (NRSV)

Rejoice always, pray without ceasing, give thanks in all circumstances; for this is the will of God in Christ Jesus for you. Do not quench the Spirit. Do not despise the words of prophets, but test everything; hold fast to what is good; abstain from every form of evil.

May the God of peace himself sanctify you entirely; and may your spirit and soul and body be kept sound and blameless at the coming of our Lord Jesus Christ. The one who calls you is faithful, and he will do this.

Philippians 4:4 – 8 (NRSV)

Rejoice in the Lord always; again I will say, Rejoice. Let your gentleness be known to everyone. The Lord is near. Do not worry about anything, but in everything by prayer and supplication with thanksgiving let your requests be made known to God. And the peace of God, which surpasses all understanding, will guard you hearts and your minds in Christ Jesus.

Reflection

These readings encourage us to reflect on how God has proven an unfailing faithfulness to us. As we consider the many graces we have received, what grace in particular has enabled us to grow the most spiritually? As an act of thanksgiving, we can write in a journal or on a slip of paper the blessing that has meant the most to us.

Following Jesus Way

Let this passage from Ephesians set the tone for our thanksgiving.

> God, who is rich in mercy, out of the great love with which he loved us even when we were dead through our trespasses, made us alive together with Christ—by grace you have been saved—and raised us up with him and seated us with him in the heavenly places in Christ Jesus, so that in the ages to come he might show the immeasurable riches of his grace in kindness toward us in Christ Jesus. For by grace you have been saved through faith, and this is not your own doing; it is the gift of God—not the result of works, so that no one may boast. For we are what he has made us, created in Christ Jesus for good works, which God prepared beforehand to be our way of life.
>
> *Ephesians 2:4–10 (NRSV)*

God has worked in our lives in wondrous ways. Oftentimes, we take for granted the gifts God gives so freely, lovingly, tenderly. Each gift, each moment of life, is too precious to let slip by.

Look for a few moments at your hands. Hold them open, palms up, on your lap or stretched out in front of you. Our hands receive so many things every day. Think of the things your hands have grasped today or in the past week: the support of a railing on the stairs, a friendly hand, a sandwich, a book, Communion…. The list is endless. Each time we open our hands, we receive a gift. Some of these gifts we have welcomed fully. Others we barely noticed. Unnoticed gifts are often never unwrapped, seen for what they are, appreciated. We can take a few moments now to pray with our hands. Let our open hands symbolize a welcoming heart ready to receive the graces God wants to give: much-needed graces that are overlooked; graces that could fill us, amaze us; graces that are waiting for us if we are open to receiving them.

God has given so much to us. Aware of the many graces we have received, we pause to reflect on the ways we have responded to the invitations hidden within each grace. How generously have we shared our gifts, especially the ones that mean the most to us? How do we share our time and our love?

Pause to reflect on the challenges you face in your everyday life, confronting them with the Word of God we have just read.

Jesus wants to give us the fullness of life. For God's gratuitous, never-ceasing forgiveness, pray:

My Lord, I am entirely the work
      of your omnipotent love.

HOUR
12

I adore you, my God, one in nature
and triune in Persons.

I thank you, because you have made me for the
happiness which lies in you and for your eternal
glory. Save me with your omnipotence, your love,
your mercy!

—*Venerable James Alberione*

Sharing Jesus' Life

When we realize how much we have received as gift
from God, we are inspired to share what we have received.
We can share the abundance of God's gifts to us first of all
by our prayers for those facing great suffering or depriva-
tion: people without faith or a relationship with Jesus;
people living in countries devastated by war; women and
children who are abused and treated as objects; families
grieving the loss of a loved one; all those who are victim-
ized by poverty, starvation, or violence; those who fight
for basic human rights; broken families; those who suffer
from illness; those who are desperately searching for meaning or purpose in their lives. Perhaps there is a story in the
news that we wish to pray for in a special way today. We
are all the Body of Christ; which suffering members do
we wish to sustain with our prayers today?

*After we have chosen a special intention, we pray the Our
Father slowly, letting the meaning of each expression of
praise or petition penetrate and expand our heart.*

HOUR
12

To conclude the hour of adoration, we can pray our own litany of thanksgiving, listing our many reasons for joy followed by a response such as, "We praise you, Lord."

As we go forth into our daily lives, we cultivate a spirit of gratitude and generosity in our hearts.

Part Three

Popular Eucharistic Prayers

"That all may have life"

In Adoration

Avoid all formalism.

This holds good for all prayer but especially for the Eucharistic Visit.

The real Visit is a spirit which pervades the whole of our time, thoughts, relationships and life.

It is a sap or life-giving current which influences everything
and communicates its spirit to the most ordinary things.

It shapes a spirituality that is lived and passed on.

It shapes the spirit of prayer which, once cultivated, changes all kinds of work into prayer….

Tell Jesus everything; if you have some troubles, if your heart is full of hope, full of the desire to be united with him….

Confide even those worries that you dare not say to anyone…tell him even if your shoe hurts.

Tell Jesus everything, with the simplicity of a child.

—*Blessed James Alberione*

Prayer of Adoration
adapted from Blessed James Alberione

Jesus, today's adoration is the meeting of my soul
and all of my being with you.
I am the creature meeting the Creator;
the disciple before the Divine Master;
the patient with the Doctor of souls;
the poor one appealing to the Rich One;
the thirsty one drinking at the Font;
the weak before the Almighty;
the tempted seeking a sure Refuge;
the blind person searching for the Light;
the friend who goes to the True Friend;
the lost sheep sought by the Divine Shepherd;
the wayward heart who finds the Way;
the unenlightened one who finds Wisdom;
the bride who finds the Spouse of the soul;
the "nothing" who finds the All;
the afflicted who finds the Consoler;
the seeker who finds life's meaning.

Prayer of Presence
Traditional, adapted

Lord, we come before you here in the Eucharist,
and we believe that you are looking at us and listening to our prayer.
You are so great and so holy, we adore you.

You have given us everything, we thank you.
We have sinned against you
and we ask your pardon with hearts full of sorrow.
You are rich in mercy; we ask you to grant us
all the graces which will help us draw closer to You.

The Eucharist and Our Daily Lives
by Karl Rahner, SJ

Come, Lord, enter my heart, you who are crucified,
who have died, who love, who are faithful, truthful,
patient and humble, you who have taken upon
yourself a slow and toilsome life in a single corner
of the world, denied by those who are your own, too
little loved by your friends, betrayed by them,
subjected to the law, made the plaything of politics
right from the very first, a refugee child, a
carpenter's son, a creature who found only barren-
ness and futility as a result of his labors, a man who
loved and who found no love in response, you who
were too exalted for those about you to understand,
you who were left desolate, who were brought to the
point of feeling yourself forsaken by God, you who
sacrificed all, who commend yourself into the hands
of your Father, you who cry: "My God, my Father,
why have your forsaken me?" I will receive you as
you are, make you the innermost law of my life, take
you as at once the burden and strength of my life.
When I receive you I accept my everyday just as it

is. I do not need to have any lofty feelings in my heart to recount to you. I can lay my everyday before you just as it is, for I receive it from you yourself, the everyday and its inward light, the everyday and its meaning, the everyday and the power to endure it, the sheer familiarity of it which becomes the hiddenness of your eternal life.

You

an ancient Celtic blessing

You are the peace of all things calm,
you are the place to hide from harm,
you are the light that shines in the dark,
you are the heart's eternal spark,
you are the door that's open wide,
you are the guest who waits inside,
you are the stranger at the door,
you are the calling of the poor,
you are the light, the truth, the way,
you are my Savior this very day.

Bread of Life

by Raymond Chapman

Bread of Life and Cup of Blessing, let our hunger and thirst for you ever grow. May we come to you in trust, and go forth to act in your name.

Into God's Care
by Women of Kenya

Lord God, I bring to you:

My sins for your forgiveness.
My hopes, my aims, my ambitions
    for your blessings.
My temptations for your strength.
My words and duties and responsibilities
    for your help.
My family, friends and all loved ones
    for your care and protection.
My sickness for your healing.

Prayer of Longing for Christ
from a tenth-century prayer to Christ

Come, true light.
Come, life eternal.
Come, hidden mystery.
Come, treasure without name.
Come, reality beyond all words.
Come, person beyond all understanding.
Come, rejoicing without end.
Come, light that knows no evening.
Come, raising up of the fallen.
Come, resurrection of the dead.

Christ Is with Us
by Pope Paul VI

Christ is truly Emmanuel, that is, "God is with us."
Day and night, he is in our midst; he dwells with us
full of grace and truth. He restores morality, nour-
ishes virtue, consoles the afflicted, strengthens the
weak. He proposes his own example to those who
come to him that they may learn to be like himself,
meek and humble of heart, and to seek not their own
interest, but the things of God.

Your Peace Floods Us
by Phivan Nguyen

Jesus,
at this moment, please come to us.
Let your peace grow in us
so anger, grief, confusion and hate
can no longer take control.
You are our Way, our Truth, and our Life—
the Way to forgive and to love even our enemy;
the Truth we live by when we follow your words;
the Life that leads to eternal life with you.
We close our eyes,
breathe deeply,
and remember that you, Jesus,
gave your life for us.
Now your light shines through us

and the darkness is vanished.
Your love embraces us,
and your peace floods us.
We are now at peace,
for you are with us.

O Sacred Banquet
Traditional

O sacred banquet, in which we receive Christ;
we remember his passion;
we are filled with grace,
and we are given a pledge of future glory, alleluia!

We Adore You
by Saint Thomas Aquinas
translated by Daughters of St. Paul

We adore you, hidden God, in this sacrament—
Christ our Savior and our King, truly present.
Humbly we come before you,
hearts completely won,
lost in wonder at the great marvels you have done.

Sense alone will fail to grasp this great mystery.
Faith and love enable our human eyes to see.
We believe all the truth
that God's own Son has shown.
Nothing can be truer than what he has made known.

On the cross was hidden your divinity.
Hidden here before us, too, is your humanity.
We in faith profess them both, one in our belief.
And we make our own the plea of the dying thief.

Thomas saw your wounds, O Lord;
these we do not see.
Yet do we confess of you: Lord and God to be.
May this faith of ours
ever grow and our hope increase.
May our burning love for you, Jesus, never cease.

O most blest memorial of Christ's sacrifice,
giver of eternal life—Bread of paradise!
You are food for our hung'ring souls;
live in us, O Lord.
Be the only goal we seek; be our sole reward.

We are cleansed, Lord, by your blood;
filled with grace and love.
One drop shed to save the world
would have been enough.
Yet you suffered and died for us, mankind lost in sin.
Oh how great a price you paid to redemption win.

Jesus, whom we now behold
veiled from human sight,
grant us what we thirst for so: that one day we might
face to face behold your vision,
bliss you have in store,
love surpassing space and time, joy forevermore.

Conversation with Jesus Master
by Blessed James Alberione

[After receiving the Eucharist]

I adore you present in me, Incarnate Word, only-begotten Son and splendor of the Father, born of Mary. I thank you, sole Master and Truth, for coming to me. With Mary I offer you to the Father: through you, with you, in you, may there be eternal praise, thanksgiving and petition for peace for all people. Enlighten my mind; make me a faithful disciple of the Church; make mine a life of faith. Give me an understanding of the Scriptures, make me your enthusiastic apostle. Let the light of your Gospel shine to the ends of the earth.

Jesus, you are the Way I want to follow: the perfect model to imitate. I want my whole life to be configured to you.

You were humble and obedient: make me similar to you.

You loved unselfishly and with a pure heart: make me similar to you.

You were poor in spirit and patient: make me similar to you.

You loved everyone and sought to bring everyone to your Father: make me similar to you.

O Jesus, my Life, my joy and source of all good, I love you. May I more generously love you and the people you came to save.

You are the vine and I am the branch; I want to remain united to you always so as to bear much fruit.

You are the fount: pour out an ever greater abundance of grace to sanctify me.

You are my head, I, your member: communicate to me your Holy Spirit with the Spirit's gifts. May your kingdom come through Mary.

Console and save all my dear ones. Bring those who have died into your presence. Assist all who share your mission of spreading the Good News. Bless the Church with many vocations to the priesthood and religious life.

For Light and Guidance

God comes, and God's ways are near to us.
God saves in history.
Each person's life, each one's history,
is the meeting place God comes to.
How satisfying to know one need not go
to the desert to meet God,
need not go to some particular spot
in the world.
God is in your own heart.

—*Oscar Romero*

Come Holy Spirit
Traditional

Come, Holy Spirit, fill the hearts of your faithful
and enkindle in them the fire of your love.
Send forth your Spirit and they shall be created;
and you shall renew the face of the earth.

Lead, Kindly Light
by John Henry Newman

Lead, kindly Light, amid the encircling gloom,
Lead thou me on.
The night is dark, and I am far from home.
Lead thou me on.
Keep thou my feet; I do not ask to see
The distant scene; one step enough for me.

I was not ever thus, nor prayed that thou
Should lead me on.
I loved to choose and see my path; but now
Lead thou me on.
I loved the garish day, and, spite of fears,
Pride ruled my will: remember not past years.

So long thy power has blest me, sure it still
Will lead me on
O'er moor and fen, o'er crag and torrent, till
The night is gone,
And with the morn, those angel faces smile
While I have loved long since, and lost awhile.

Prayer for the Gifts of the Holy Spirit
by Blessed James Alberione

Divine Holy Spirit,
eternal Love of the Father and of the Son,
I adore you, I thank you, I love you
and I ask your forgiveness
for all the times I have sinned against you
and against my neighbor.
Descend with many graces
on those ordained as bishops and priests,
on those consecrated as men and women religious,
on those who receive the sacrament of Confirmation.
Be light, sanctity, zeal for them.
To you, Spirit of truth,
I dedicate my mind, imagination and memory.
Enlighten me.
Bring me to fuller knowledge of Jesus Christ,
and a deeper understanding of the Gospel and the
teaching of the Church.
Increase in me the gifts of wisdom, knowledge,
understanding and counsel.
To you, sanctifying Spirit,
I dedicate my will.
Guide me, make me faithful in living fully
the commandments and my vocation.
Grant me the gifts of fortitude and holy fear of God.
To you, life-giving Spirit,
I dedicate my heart.

Guard me from evil; pour on me an always greater
abundance of your life.
Bring to completion your work in me.
Grant me the gift of piety. Amen.

Veni, Sancte Spíritus
Traditional

Come, Holy Spirit, Creator, come,
from your bright heavenly throne;
come, take possession of our souls,
and make them all your own.

You who are called the Paraclete,
best gift of God above;
the living spring, the living fire,
sweet unction and true love.

You who are sevenfold in your grace,
finger of God's right hand,
his promise, teaching little ones
to speak and understand.

O guide our minds with your blest light,
with love our hearts inflame
and with your strength which ne'er decays,
confirm our mortal frame.

Far from us drive our hellish foe,
true peace unto us bring;
and through all perils lead us safe
beneath your sacred wing.

Through you may we the Father know,
through you, the eternal Son,
and you, the Spirit of them both—
thrice-blessed three in one.

All glory to the Father be,
and to his risen Son,
the like to you, great Paraclete,
while endless ages run. Amen.

Come Holy Spirit
by Saint Mary Magdalen dei Pazzi

Come Holy Spirit.
Let the precious pearl of the Father
and the Word's delight come.
Spirit of truth,
you are the reward of the saints,
the comforter of souls,
light in the darkness,
riches to the poor,
treasure to lovers,
food for the hungry,
comfort to the wanderer;
to sum up,
you are the one in whom
all treasures are contained.

Come!

As you descended on Mary,
that the Word might become flesh,
work in us through grace
as you worked in her through nature and grace.

Come!

Food of every chaste thought,
fountain of all mercy,
sum of all purity.

Come!

Consume in us
whatever prevents us from
being consumed in you. Amen.

Acts of Faith

Have faith and do not doubt; this Jesus is
infinitely faithful to his promises.

—Blessed James Alberione

The Apostles' Creed
Traditional

I believe in God, the Father almighty, creator of
heaven and earth.
I believe in Jesus Christ, his only Son, our Lord.
He was conceived by the power of the Holy Spirit
and born of the Virgin Mary.
He suffered under Pontius Pilate, was crucified,
died and was buried.
He descended to the dead.
On the third day he arose again.
He ascended into heaven, and is seated at the right
hand of the Father.
He will come again to judge the living and the dead.
I believe in the Holy Spirit, the holy Catholic
Church, the communion of saints,
the forgiveness of sins, the resurrection of the body,
and life everlasting. Amen.

Act of Faith
Traditional

O my God, I firmly believe that you are one God in
three Divine Persons, Father, Son and Holy Spirit. I
believe that your Divine Son become man and died
for our sins, and that he will come to judge the living
and the dead. I believe these and all the truths which

the holy Catholic Church teaches, because you have revealed them, who can neither deceive nor be deceived. Amen.

Short Acts of Faith

My Lord and my God!

I can do all things in him who strengthens me.

Philippians 4:13

I believe, Lord; help my unbelief!

My Lord, I believe you are looking on me with love.

We Adore You, Jesus Truth
by Blessed James Alberione

Jesus, Divine Master, we adore you as the Word Incarnate sent by the Father to teach us life-giving truths. You are uncreated Truth, the only Master. You alone have words of eternal life. We thank you for having gifted us with the light of reason and faith, and for having called us to the light of glory in heaven. We believe in you and the teachings of the Church, and we pray that your Word may enlighten our minds. Master, show us the treasures of your wisdom; let us know the Father; make us your true disciples. Increase our faith so that we may reach eternal life in heaven.

Prayer of Faith in Darkness
by Saint Jane Frances de Chantal

O Lord God,
I am in a barren land,
parched and cracked by the violence
of the north wind and the cold.
But as you see,
I believe in you.
You will send me both dew and warmth
when I am ready.

Prayer to Obtain Faith
by Pope Paul VI

Lord, I believe; I wish to believe in you.

Lord, let my faith be full and unreserved, and let it penetrate my thoughts, my way of judging divine things and human things.

Lord, let my faith be free; that is, let it have my personal adherence. Let me accept the renunciations and duties that faith entails. May the expression of my faith be the culminating point of my personality: I believe in you, Lord.

Lord, let my faith be certain, strong, joyful. May I live in true friendship with you. In all that I do and experience, may my life be a continual search for you, a testimony to you, a nourishment of hope in you.

Acts of Trust

The present moment alone is important….
Entrust the past to the mercy of God, entrust
the future to his providence, and entrust
everything to his love.

—*Francis Xavier Nguyen Van Thuan*

Act of Hope
Traditional

O my God, relying on your almighty power and infinite goodness and promises, I hope to obtain pardon of my sins, the help of your grace, and life everlasting, through the merits of Jesus Christ, my Lord and Redeemer. Amen.

Prayer of Surrender
by Blessed Charles de Foucauld

Father, I abandon myself into your hands;
do with me what you will.
Whatever you may do, I thank you;
I am ready for all, I accept all.
Let only your will be done in me,
and in all your creatures.
I wish no more than this, O Lord.

Into your hands I commend myself;
I offer myself to you with all the love
of my heart,
for I love you, Lord,
and so need to give myself,
to surrender myself into your hands
without reserve,
and with boundless confidence
because you are my Father.

Act of Trust in the Divine Master
by Giovannamaria Carrara, FSP

The Master is here in my personal story with its lights and shadows. Jesus is calling me to accept my story as he does and to explore the vast horizons of his peace.

The Master is here in my work and in my service.

The Master is here in my family and my community. He is calling me to dialog and trust. He is calling me to live his love.

The Master is here in the Church, in its efforts for evangelization and service, in the Liturgy which pulsates with the power of the Holy Spirit. Jesus is calling me to contemplate his mysteries as they unfold throughout the liturgical year.

The Master is here in the poor and the oppressed, in those who suffer or have lost their way, in those who need the light of my faith and the gift of my love.

The Master is here in the depths of my heart. He is calling me to open the door to him so that he might dwell within me, his chosen home.

Lines Written in Her Breviary
by Saint Teresa of Avila

Let nothing disturb thee,
Nothing affright thee;

All things are passing;
God never changeth;

Patient endurance
Attaineth to all things;
Who God possesseth
In nothing is wanting;
Alone God sufficeth.

Prayer for Hope
by Karl Rahner, sj

Son of the Father, Christ who lives in us, you are our hope of glory. Live in us, bringing our life under the laws of your life, make our life like to yours. Live in me, pray in me, suffer in me, more I do not ask. For if I have you I am rich; those who find you have found the power and the victory of their life. Amen.

We Adore You, Jesus Way
by Blessed James Alberione

Jesus, Divine Master, we adore you as the Beloved of the Father, the sole Way to him. We thank you because you showed us how to live a holy life, making yourself our model. We contemplate you throughout your earthly life. You have invited us to follow your example. We want to follow your teachings, treating everyone with love and respect. Draw us to yourself, so that by following in your footsteps and practicing self-sacrifice, we may seek only your will. Increase hope in us and the desire to be similar to you, so that we may rejoice to hear your words, "Come...inherit the kingdom prepared for you from the foundation of the world.... Just as you did it to one of the least of these... you did it to me" (Matthew 25:34, 40).

When We Most Need You
by Angela Ashwin

When all feels dark
and hope is hard to find,
remind us, loving God,
that you are closest to us
at the points where we most need you.
For nothing,
nothing at all,
can take us away from your love
in Christ Jesus. Amen.

Help Me, Who Am Alone
from the Book of Esther

My Lord, our King, you alone are God.
Help me, who am alone
and have no help but you,
for I am taking my life in my hand....
O God, more powerful than all,

hear the voice of those in despair.
Save us from the power of the wicked,
and deliver me from my fear.

Psalm 131

O Lord, my heart is not lifted up,
my eyes are not raised too high;

I do not occupy myself with things
too great and too marvelous for me.

But I have calmed and quieted my soul,
like a weaned child with its mother;
my soul is like the weaned child that is with me.

O Israel, hope in the Lord
from this time on and forevermore.

Heart of Love
by Saint Margaret Mary Alocoque

O Heart of love,
I place my trust entirely in you.
Though I fear all things from my weakness,
I hope all things from your goodness!

With Praise and Thanksgiving

My being…rejoices in God my Savior.
—*Mary, the Mother of Jesus (Luke 1:47)*

Psalm 8

O LORD, our Sovereign,
how majestic is your name in all the earth!

You have set your glory above the heavens.
Out of the mouths of babes and infants

you have founded a bulwark because of your foes,
to silence the enemy and the avenger.

When I look at your heavens,
    the work of your fingers,
the moon and the stars that you have established;

what are human beings that you are mindful of them,
mortals that you care for them?

Yet you have made them a little lower than God,
and crowned them with glory and honor.

You have given them dominion over the works of
    your hands;
you have put all things under their feet,

all sheep and oxen,
and also the beasts of the field,

the birds of the air, and the fish of the sea,
whatever passes along the paths of the seas.

O LORD, our Sovereign,
how majestic is your name in all the earth!

Psalm 146

Praise the LORD!

Praise the LORD, O my soul!

I will praise the LORD as long as I live
    I will sing praises to my God all my life long.

Do not put your trust in princes,
    in mortals, in whom there is no help.

When their breath departs, they return to the earth;
    on that very day their plans perish.

Happy are those whose help is the God of Jacob,
    whose hope is in the LORD their God,

who made heaven and earth,
    the sea, and all that is in them;

who keeps faith forever;
    who executes justice for the oppressed;
    who gives food to the hungry.

The LORD sets the prisoners free;
    the LORD opens the eyes of the blind.

The LORD lifts up those who are bowed down;
    the LORD loves the righteous.

The LORD watches over the strangers;
    he upholds the orphan and the widow,
    but the way of the wicked he brings to ruin.

The LORD will reign forever,
    your God, O Zion, for all generations.

Praise the LORD!

Canticle from Saint Paul's Letter to the Philippians
Philippians 2:5–11 (NRSV)

Let the same mind be in you that was in Christ Jesus,

who, though he was in the form of God,
    did not regard equality with God
    as something to be exploited,

but emptied himself,
    taking the form of a slave,
    being born in human likeness.

And being found in human form,
    he humbled himself
    and became obedient to the point of death—
    even death on a cross.

Therefore God also highly exalted him
    and gave him the name
    that is above every name,

so that at the name of Jesus
    every knee should bend,
    in heaven and on earth and under the earth,

and every tongue should confess
    that Jesus Christ is Lord,
    to the glory of God the Father.

Hymn to Christ
by Pope John Paul II

Christ of our sufferings,
Christ of our sacrifices,
Christ of our Gethsemane,
Christ of our difficult transformations.
Christ of our faithful service to our neighbor,
Christ of our pilgrimage,
Christ of our community,
Christ our Redeemer,
Christ our Brother! Amen.

A Grateful Heart
by George Herbert

Thou hast given so much to me,
Give one thing more—a grateful heart;
Not thankful when it pleaseth me,
As if thy blessings had spare days;
But such a heart, whose pulse may be Thy praise.

Te Deum
Traditional

We praise you, O God;
    we acknowledge you to be the Lord.
All the earth worships you, the everlasting Father.

To you all the angels, the heavens,
    and all the Powers,
  the cherubim and seraphim cry out
    without ceasing:

Holy, holy, holy Lord God of hosts!
  The majesty of your glory fills the heavens
    and the earth.

The glorious choir of apostles,
    the admirable company of prophets,
  the white-robed army of martyrs praise you.

Through the world the holy Church testifies to you:
  the Father, whose glory is beyond
    our comprehension,
  your adorable, true and only Son,
  and the Holy Spirit, the Paraclete.

You, O Christ, are the king of glory.
  You are the eternal Son of the Father.

You did not disdain a virgin's womb to redeem man.
  You overcame death, and opened the kingdom
    of heaven for the faithful.

Now you are seated at the right hand of God,
    in the glory of the Father.
  We believe that you will come again as Judge.

Help your servants, whom you have redeemed
    with your precious blood.
  Number them among your saints
    in everlasting glory.

Save your people, O Lord,
      and bless your inheritance,
   and govern them and keep them safe forever.

Through each day we bless you.
   And praise your name forever;
      indeed, forever and ever.
   Grant, O Lord, to keep us without sin this day.

Have mercy on us, O Lord; have mercy on us.
   Let your mercy be upon us, O Lord,
      as we have trusted in you.
   In your mercy, O Lord, I have trusted;
      let me not be put to shame forever.

For Mercy

The greater my unworthiness,
the more abundant God's mercy.

—*Saint Elizabeth Seton*

Wellspring of Mercy
by Joyce Rupp

Wellspring of Mercy, you welcome me home.
You understand my human failings.
You embrace me in my incompleteness.
You help me move on from failures and defeat.
How good and gracious is your kindness to me.

Too Late Have I Loved You
by Saint Augustine

Too late have I loved you, O Beauty so ancient and
so new, too late have I loved you! Behold, you were
within me, while I was outside: it was there that
I sought you, and, a deformed creature, rushed
headlong upon these things of beauty which you
have made. You were with me, but I was not with
you. They kept me far from you, those fair things
which, if they were not in you, would not exist at all.
You have called to me, and have cried out, and have
shattered my deafness. You have blazed forth with
light, and have shone upon me, and you have put
my blindness to flight! You have sent forth fra-
grance, and I have drawn in my breath, and I pant
after you. I have tasted you, and I hunger and thirst
after you. You have touched me, and I have burned
for your peace.

Be Mindful of Your Mercy
Psalm 25:4 – 7

Make me to know your ways, O Lord;
 teach me your paths.

Lead me in your truth, and teach me,
 for you are the God of my salvation;
 for you I wait all day long.

Be mindful of your mercy, O Lord,
 and of your steadfast love,
 for they have been from of old.

Do not remember the sins of my youth
  or my transgressions;
 according to your steadfast love remember me
 for your goodness' sake, O Lord!

Psalm 130

Out of the depths I cry to you, O LORD.
 LORD, hear my voice!

Let your ears be attentive
 to the voice of my supplications!

If you, O LORD, should mark iniquities,
 LORD, who could stand?

But there is forgiveness with you,
 so that you may be revered.

I wait for the LORD, my soul waits,
    and in his word I hope;

my soul waits for the LORD
    more than those who watch for the morning,
    more than those who watch for the morning.

O Israel, hope in the LORD!
    For with the LORD there is steadfast love,
    and with him is great power to redeem.

It is he who will redeem Israel
    from all its iniquities.

In Commitment and Discipleship

The [Eucharistic] Visit is the practice
which guides and influences our whole life....

It draws together the fruits of all other practices and brings them to fruition.

It is the great means for living Jesus Christ.

It is the great means for putting childhood
aside and forming a personality in Christ.

It is the secret for our transformation in Christ.

It is experiencing the relationship of Jesus with
his Father and with humanity.

It is the guarantee of perseverance.

—Blessed James Alberione

Daily Offering
Traditional

Divine Heart of Jesus, through the Immaculate Heart of Mary, I offer you all my prayers, works, joys and sufferings of this day, in reparation for sins, and for the salvation of all men and women, according to the special intentions of the Pope, in the grace of the Holy Spirit, for the glory of the heavenly Father. Amen.

A Morning Offering
by Maryland Province Jesuits

O Jesus, I come before you
at the beginning of this day.

I gaze at your face,
I look upon your side
pierced by the lance.

Your wounded heart speaks to me
of God's love poured out for us.

Take, Lord, and receive my heart:
the words of faith that I speak,
the works of justice I would do,
my joys and sufferings.

When I come to the Eucharistic table,
gather my offerings to your own
for the life of the world.

At the end of the day,
place me with Mary, your mother,
and for her sake take me to your heart. Amen.

To the Divine Master
by Blessed James Alberione

Master, your life traces out the way for me. Your
truth confirms and enlightens my steps. Your grace
sustains and comforts me on my journey toward
heaven.

To Jesus Crucified
Traditional

Behold, my beloved and good Jesus,
I kneel before you,
asking you most earnestly
to engrave upon my heart
a deep and lively faith, hope and charity,
with true repentance for my sins,
and a firm resolve to make amends.
As I reflect upon your five wounds,
and dwell upon them with deep compassion
    and grief,
I recall, good Jesus, the words the prophet David
    spoke long ago:
they have pierced my hands and my feet,
they have counted all my bones!

We Adore You Living in the Church
by Blessed James Alberione

Jesus, Divine Master, we adore you living in the
Church, the Mystical Body of Christ, through which
you bring us to eternal life. We thank you for having
joined us together as members of the Church, in
which you continue to be for humanity the Way, the
Truth and the Life. We ask that those who do not
believe may receive the gift of faith, that those who
are separated may be brought into full communion,
and that all people be united in faith, in a common
hope, in charity. Assist the Church and its leaders;
sustain the People of God. Lord Jesus, our wish is
yours: that there be one fold under one Shepherd, so
that we may all be together in heaven.

Prayer for Holiness of Life
by Saint Catherine of Siena

Godhead! Godhead!
Eternal Godhead!
I proclaim and do not deny it:
You are a peaceful sea
in which the spirit feeds and is nourished
while resting in you.
Unite our will with your will
in love's affection and union
so that we will want for nothing
other than becoming holy.

Act of Offering to the Most Holy Trinity
by Blessed James Alberione

Divine Trinity,
Father, Son and Holy Spirit,
present and active in the Church
and in the depths of my soul,
I adore you, I thank you, I love you!

Through the hands of Mary most holy,
I offer myself entirely to you
for life and for eternity.
To you, heavenly Father, I offer myself as your child.
To you, Jesus Master, I offer myself as your disciple.
To you, Holy Spirit, I offer myself as a "living
    temple" to be consecrated and sanctified.

Mary, Mother of the Church and my mother,
who dwells in the presence of the Blessed Trinity,
teach me to live, through the liturgy
    and the sacraments,
in ever more intimate union
    with the three divine Persons,
so that my whole life may be
a glory to the Father, to the Son,
    and to the Holy Spirit. Amen.

The Mysteries of the Rosary

Joyful Mysteries

[Usually prayed on Mondays and Saturdays]

1. The Annunciation to the Blessed Virgin Mary
   (Luke 1:38)
2. Mary Visits Her Cousin Elizabeth (Luke 1:45)
3. The Birth of Jesus at Bethlehem (Luke 2:7)
4. The Presentation of Jesus in the Temple
   (Luke 2:22)
5. The Finding of the Child Jesus in the Temple
   (Luke 2:49)

Luminous Mysteries

[Usually prayed on Thursdays]

1. John Baptizes Jesus in the Jordan (Matthew 3:17)
2. Jesus Reveals His Glory at the Wedding of Cana
   (John 2:5)
3. Jesus Proclaims the Kingdom of God and Calls Us
   to Conversion (Mark 1:15)
4. The Transfiguration of Jesus (Luke 9:35)
5. Jesus Gives Us the Eucharist (John 6:54)

Sorrowful Mysteries

[Usually prayed on Tuesdays and Fridays]

1. Jesus Prays in the Garden of Gethsemane (Luke 22:44)
2. Jesus is Scourged at the Pillar (John 19:1)
3. Jesus is Crowned with Thorns (Mark 15:17)
4. Jesus Carries the Cross to Calvary (John 19:17)
5. Jesus Dies for Our Sins (John 19:26–27)

Glorious Mysteries

[Usually prayed on Wednesdays and Sundays]

1. Jesus Rises from the Dead (John 20:19)
2. Jesus Ascends into Heaven (Mark 16:19)
3. The Holy Spirit Descends on the Apostles (Acts 2:4)
4. Mary is Assumed into Heaven (Luke 1:48–49)
5. Mary is Crowned Queen of Heaven and Earth (2 Timothy 2:12)

Marian Prayer
by Pope John Paul II

Mother of the Redeemer,
with great joy we call you blessed.
In order to carry out his plan of salvation,
God the Father chose you before the creation of
    the world.
You believed in his love and obeyed his word.
The Son of God desired you for his Mother
when he became man to save the human race.
You received him with ready obedience
    and undivided heart.
The Holy Spirit loved you as his mystical spouse
and he filled you with singular gifts.
You allowed yourself to be led by his hidden and
    powerful action.

At the beginning of the third Christian Millennium,
we entrust to you the Church which acknowledges
    and invokes you as Mother.
On earth you preceded the Church
    in the pilgrimage of faith:
comfort us in our difficulties and trials,
and make us always the sign and instrument
    of intimate union with God
and of the unity of the whole human race.

To you, Mother of the human family
    and of the nations,

we confidently entrust the whole of humanity,
with its hopes and fears.
Do not let it lack the light of true wisdom.
Guide its steps in the ways of peace.
Enable all to meet Christ,
the Way and the Truth and the Life.
Sustain us, O Virgin Mary,
on our journey of faith
and obtain for us the grace of eternal salvation.
O clement, O loving, O sweet Mother of God
and our Mother, Mary!

For Strength, Grace, Growth

Our life—to be eucharistic—must be wheat—
seed and soil—light and darkness,
growth and grinding—
rhythm and season—now barren,
now blooming,
now barren again—
eruptive force of faith and hoping.

—*Jane Walker, OP*

For Protection and Enlightenment
by Saint Patrick

May the strength of God pilot us.
May the power of God preserve us.
May the wisdom of God instruct us.
May the hand of God protect us.
May the way of God direct us.
May the shield of God defend us.
May the hosts of God protect us
Now and always.

Abide with Me
by H.F. Lyte

Abide with me; fast falls the eventide;
The darkness deepens; Lord with me abide;
When other helpers fail, and comforts flee,
Help of the helpless, O abide with me.

Swift to its close ebbs out life's little day;
Earth's joys grow dim, its glories pass away;
Change and decay in all around I see;
O thou who changest not, abide with me.

Hold thou thy cross before my closing eyes;
Shine through the gloom, and point me to the skies;
Heaven's morning breaks,
    and earth's vain shadows flee;
In life, in death, O Lord, abide with me.

Beloved of My Soul
by Joyce Rupp

Beloved of my soul, I long to embrace you.
I savor the love which you offer to me.
I accept the challenges.
I receive the truths meant to transform me.
Grant me the courage not to run away.
I let go of my expectations and timetable.
May this solitude influence the totality of my life.

A Better Resurrection
by Christina Rossetti

I have no wit, no words, no tears;
My heart within me like a stone
Is numbed too much for hopes or fears;
Look right, look left, I dwell alone;
I lift mine eyes, but dimmed with grief
No everlasting hills I see;
My life is in the falling leaf:
O Jesus, quicken me.

My life is like a faded leaf,
My harvest dwindled to a husk
Truly my life is void and brief
And tedious in the barren dusk;
My life is like a frozen thing,
No bud nor greenness can I see:

Yet rise it shall—the sap of Spring;
O Jesus, rise in me.

My life is like a broken bowl,
A broken bowl that cannot hold
One drop of water for my soul
Or cordial in the searching cold;
Cast in the fire the perished thing,
Melt and remold it, till it be
A royal cup for him my King
O Jesus, drink of me.

Memorare
by Saint Bernard of Clairvaux

Remember, most gracious Virgin Mary,
never was it heard
that anyone who turned to you for help
was left unaided.
Inspired by this confidence,
though burdened by my sins,
I run to your protection,
for you are my mother.
Mother of the Word of God,
do not despise my words of pleading
but be merciful and hear my prayer.
Amen.

Acts of Love

This is the very essence of prayer:

It is not we who address God, but God who
    addresses us.

Prayer exposes to God what we are, all
    our…pains, our weakness.

God always sees our heart, seeing there what
    we have not yet seen ourselves:

God alone truly knows us, and whatever our
self-love, God's love is greater.

Nothing can put God off, no sin, no malice.
God loves us with total affection.
But in prayer we surrender to this love.
We actively open ourselves and allow him,
desire him, to flood us with his presence.

—Sister Wendy Beckett

Act of Love
Traditional

O my God, I love you above all things, with my whole heart and soul, because you are all-good and worthy of all love. I love my neighbor as myself for the love of you. I forgive all who have injured me, and I ask pardon of all whom I have injured.

Psalm 63

O God, you are my God, I seek you,
    my soul thirsts for you;

my flesh faints for you,
    as in a dry and weary land
        where there is no water.

So I have looked upon you in the sanctuary,
    beholding your power and glory.

Because your steadfast love is better than life,
    my lips will praise you.

So I will bless you as long as I live;
    I will lift up my hands and call on your name.

My soul is satisfied as with a rich feast,
    and my mouth praises you with joyful lips

when I think of you on my bed,
    and meditate on you in the watches of the night;

for you have been my help,
    and in the shadows of your wings I sing for joy.

My soul clings to you;
    your right hand upholds me.

Thou Art Life
by Christina Rossetti

Lord, Thou art life, though I be dead:
Love's fire Thou art, however cold I be:
Nor heaven have I, nor place to lay my head,
Nor home, but Thee.

Live in Us, Jesus
by Blessed James Alberione

Jesus, Divine Master, we adore you as the only-begotten Son of God, who came on earth to give abundant life to humanity. We thank you because by your death on the cross, you give us life through Baptism and you nourish us in the Eucharist and in the other sacraments. Live in us, O Jesus, with the outpouring of the Holy Spirit, so that we may love you with our whole mind, strength and heart, and love our neighbor as ourselves for love of you. Increase charity in us, so that one day we may all be united with you in the eternal happiness of heaven.

Of Disciples in the World

How often do we ponder this problem:
Humanity is like a great river
   flowing into eternity.
Where, how and toward what goal
   is humanity heading,
this humanity which is always renewing itself
   on the face of the earth?…
There is no greater wealth that we can
   offer our world than Jesus Christ.
The world needs Jesus Master,
   Way, Truth and Life.

—Blessed James Alberione

Prayer for the Needs of Others
by Saint Anselm

God of love, whose compassion never fails,
we bring you the sufferings of the world;
the needs of the homeless,
the cries of prisoners,
the pains of the sick and injured,
the sorrow of the bereaved,
the helplessness of the elderly and weak.
According to their needs and your great mercy,
strengthen and relieve them
in Jesus Christ our Lord.

Prayer of St. Francis
Traditional

Lord, make me an instrument of your peace:
where there is hatred, let me sow love;
where there is discord, harmony;
where there is injury, pardon;
where there is error, truth;
where there is doubt, faith;
where there is despair, hope;
where there is darkness, light;
where there is sadness, joy.

Divine Master,
grant that I may not so much seek
to be consoled as to console;

to be understood, as to understand;
to be loved, as to love.
For it is in giving that we receive;
it is in forgetting self that we find ourselves;
it is in pardoning that we are pardoned;
and it is in dying that we are born to eternal life.

In Our Daily Living
by Gloria Bordeghini

Lord of the world and of peace,
help us to unite these two words
in our daily life.
Peace in the world and peace in our hearts—
this we ask of you, Lord,
for if there is to be peace in the world,
there must be peace in our hearts.
Remove from us hate and rancor
and everything that impedes
a serene and happy way of life.
Give us your peace, O Lord,
the peace that the world often
does not understand or value,
but without which,
the world cannot live.

Praying the Beatitudes
by Marie Paul Curley, FSP

Lord, give me poverty of spirit, so that I always
remember that your kingdom is my true home.

Comfort me in my sorrows, Lord.
Give me compassion for others who mourn.

Give me a meek heart;
empower me to further your kingdom here on earth.

May I hunger and thirst to do your will, Lord;
I trust I will find fulfillment only in you.

Lord, give me a merciful heart,
and surround me with your mercy
when I need it most and trust in it least.

Purify my heart, Lord,
so that I may see your presence everywhere,
and one day see you face to face.

May I bring your peace everywhere I go.

Lord, give me strength, courage and perseverance
when I am persecuted for doing good.
Grant me a joyful entrance into the kingdom
of heaven.

Prayer to Mary
by Mother Teresa

Mary—
give us your heart
so beautiful,
so pure,
so immaculate,
your heart so full of love and humility,
that we may be able to receive and carry Jesus
as you received and carried him,
to others.
You are a cause of joy to us
because you gave us Jesus—
help us to be a cause of joy to others,
giving only Jesus
to all those with whom we come in contact.

May We Radiate You
by Blessed James Alberione

Jesus, Divine Master, we adore you with the angels
who sang the reasons for your incarnation: glory to
God and peace to all people. We thank you for
having called us to share in your saving mission.
Enkindle in us your flame of love for God and for all
humanity. Live in us so that we may radiate you
through our prayer, suffering and work, as well as by
word, example and deed. Send good laborers into

your harvest. Enlighten preachers, teachers, writers;
infuse in them the Holy Spirit and the Spirit's seven
gifts. Come, Master and Lord! Teach and reign,
through Mary, Mother, Teacher and Queen.

Open Us, O Lord
by Women of Canada

Lord, open our eyes,
    that we may see you in our brothers and sisters.
Lord, open our ears,
    that we may hear the cries from the hungry,
    the cold,
    the frightened, the oppressed.
Lord, open our hands,
    that we may reach out to all who are in need.
Lord, open our hearts,
    that we may love each other as you love us.

God of Love
by Saint Teresa of Avila

God of love, help us to remember
that Christ has no body now on earth but ours,
no hands but ours, no feet but ours.
Ours are the eyes to see the needs of the world.
Ours are the hands with which
    to bless everyone now.

Ours are the feet with which he is
    to go about doing good.

New Prayer of Saint Francis
by Melba Grace Lobaton

Lord Jesus, give us an awareness
    of the massive forces threatening our world.
Where there is armed conflict,
    let us stretch out our arms to our brothers
        and sisters.
Where there is abundance,
    let there be simple lifestyles and sharing.
Where there is poverty,
    let there be dignity and constant striving
        for justice.
Where there is selfish ambition,
    let there be humble service.
Where there is injustice,
    let there be atonement.
Where there is despair,
    let there be hope in the Good News.
Where there are wounds of division,
    let there be unity and wholeness.

Help us to be committed to the building
        of your kingdom,
    not seeking to be cared for, but to care;
    not expecting to be served, but to serve others;

not desiring material security,
but placing our security in your love.
For it is only in loving imitation of you, Lord,
that we can discover the healing springs of life
to bring about new birth on our earth
and hope for the world. Amen.

Take My Life
by Frances Ridley Havergal

Take my life, and let it be
Consecrated, Lord, to thee.
Take my moments and my days;
Let them flow in ceaseless praise.
Take my hands, and let them move
At the impulse of thy love.
Take my feet and let them be
Swift and beautiful for thee.

Take my voice, and let me sing,
Always, only, for my King.
Take my lips, and let them be
Filled with messages from thee.
Take my silver and my gold;
Not a mite would I withhold.
Take my intellect, and use
Every power as thou shalt choose.

Take my will, and make it thine;
It shall be no longer mine.

Take my heart, it is thine own;
It shall be thy royal throne.
Take my love; my Lord, I pour
At thy feet its treasure-store.
Take myself, and I will be
Ever, only, all for thee.

A Communicator's Prayer
by Daughters of St. Paul, India

Lord, make me an instrument of your grace.
Where there is ignorance, let me bring inspiration;
Where there is prejudice, understanding;
Where there is weariness, strength;
Where there is ugliness, beauty;
Where there is loneliness, companionship;
Where there is sadness, joy;
Where there is fear, courage;
Where there is doubt, faith;
Where there is hatred, love.
Lord, fill my mind with your truth,
     my heart with your love,
     my whole being with your Spirit.
Grant me the supreme gift
     of forgetfulness of self in service of others,
     and make your mission mine.

The following pages are provided for you to write your own favorite prayers.

Notes

1. *Lumen gentium,* n. 11.

2. Father Alberione founded the Society of Saint Paul and the Daughters of Saint Paul, who proclaim the Gospel through the media of social communication; the Pious Disciples of the Divine Master, who are dedicated to the liturgical apostolate; the Sisters of the Good Shepherd, who dedicate themselves to pastoral work; and the Sisters of Mary, Queen of Apostles, who work to promote and guide vocations to the priestly and religious life.

3. The secular institutes Alberione founded include: the Institute of Jesus the Priest for diocesan priests, the Institute of Saint Gabriel the Archangel for lay men, the Institute of Mary Most Holy of the Annunciation for lay women, and the Institute of the Holy Family for married couples.

4. Alberione, *Thoughts,* p. 141.

5. Alberione, *Following of Christ the Master,* p. 104.

6. In Alberione's words: "Devotion to Jesus Master sums up and completes all devotions. In fact, it presents Jesus Truth in whom to believe; Jesus Way who is to be followed; Jesus Life in whom we should participate... Speaking of Jesus Master, we must keep in mind a much broader sense. He not only communicates knowledge, but he also transfuses his life into the disciples, making them similar to himself. He develops the divine life in them and guides them to eternal life" (Alberione, *Following of Christ the Master,* p. 23).

7. "Ordinary teachers are able to pass on some knowledge, or principles; they are able to give advice, and so on. Jesus, instead, is the Teacher [Master] of the most necessary knowledge; he is the sure guide to eternal life; and he has grace, which is absolutely necessary for the spiritual life" (Alberione, *Ut Perfectus Sit Homo Dei,* IV, 191).

8. Father Alberione wrote: "If one then moves on to the study of Saint Paul, one finds the disciple whose knowledge of the Divine Master is complete; he lives the whole Christ; he scrutinizes in depth the mysteries of his doctrine, of his heart, of his sanctity, and of his humanity and divinity: he sees him as Healer, Victim, Priest; he presents the whole Christ to us as he had already proclaimed himself to be: Way, Truth, and Life…. This perspective encompasses the whole Jesus Christ; through this devotion Jesus Christ completely embraces and conquers the human person" (Alberione, *Abundantes Divitiae Gratiae Suae,* n. 159–160).

9. "We honor Jesus Master, who made himself our wisdom, by placing ourselves humbly at his feet; by listening to what he left us in the Gospel and communicates to us through the Church; by accepting and believing all his teachings; by repeating to him with Saint Peter: 'You have the message of eternal life, and we believe; we know that you are the Holy One of God'" (Alberione, *Following of Christ the Master,* p. 29).

10. Alberione, *Prayers of the Pauline Family,* p. 214.

11. Cf. Pope Paul VI, *Evangelii nuntiandi,* n. 27.

12. "Jesus willed to be the first one to live the life that we should live; he willed to be the first one to walk the road which would lead us to the Father…. He made himself our Way to the Father, becoming our mediator and our brother…. From this derives the absolute necessity for us to imitate Jesus our model; to make ours his adoration, his thanksgiving, his reparation, his petitions" (Alberione, *Following of Christ the Master,* p. 29).

13. Alberione, *Until Christ Be Formed in You,* p. 37

14. "We honor Jesus Life by asking him for the abundance of his life, his grace, his sanctity. In the presence of the magnificent virtue and sanctity which we discover in the life of the Master, we feel the necessity of resembling him and of praying for his help, and Jesus, called to accomplish in us his most ardent desire, will grant us the abundance of his Spirit, who will work in us 'until Christ is formed' in us" (Alberione, *Following of Christ the Master,* p. 29).

15. Pope John Paul II, General Audience of March 12, 1997.

16. The Servant of God, Venerable Thecla Merlo (1894–1964), co-founded the Daughters of Saint Paul with Father James Alberione in 1915, eventually becoming the Congregation's first Superior General. Mother Thecla Merlo was a close collaborator in many of Father Alberione's apostolic efforts, and her faith and courage led the Daughters of Saint Paul forward in what was a very unusual apostolate for women at that time in the Church: evangelizing with the media.

Bibliography

Alberione, Blessed James. *Abundantes Divitiae Gratiae Suae* (Charismatic History of the Pauline Family). Rome: St. Paul's, 1998.

―――. *Following Christ the Master in the Intuition of the Founder.* Boston: Daughters of Saint Paul.

―――. *Prayers of the Pauline Family.* Boston: Daughters of Saint Paul, 1991.

―――. *Thoughts by Venerable James Alberione.* Boston: Daughters of Saint Paul, 1974.

―――. *Ut Perfectus Sit Homo Dei.* Rome: Saint Paul's, 1998.

―――. *Until Christ Be Formed in You.* Boston: Daughters of Saint Paul, 1983.

Rolfo, Luigi. *James Alberione: Apostle for Our Times.* Bro. Salvatore Paglieri, SSP, translator. Staten Island, NY: Society of Saint Paul, 1987.

Church Documents

Evangelii nuntiandi (On Evangelization in the Modern World), by Pope Paul VI. Daughters of Saint Paul, Boston, 1975.

Lumen gentium (Dogmatic Constitution on the Church), Second Vatican Council. Daughters of Saint Paul, Boston, 1965, 1998.

Acknowledgments

Page 32: Picture of Christ washing Peter's feet, Fußwaschung © Sieger Köder.

Page 143: "The Eucharist and Our Daily Lives"; and page 144: "Prayer for Hope"; in *Prayers of a Lifetime* by Karl Rahner. Copyright © 1984, The Crossroad Publishing Company, New York, NY. All Rights Reserved. Used with permission of the Crossroad Publishing Company, New York.

Page 144: "You"; page 146: "Your Peace Floods Us"; page 165: "When We Most Need You"; page 196: "In Our Daily Living"; and page 200: "New Prayer of St. Francis"; in *A World on Its Knees.* Copyright © 2001, Daughters of St. Paul, Pauline Books & Media, Boston, MA. All Rights Reserved.

Page 144: "Bread of Life," in *Lenten Days, Lenten Grace* by Raymond Chapman. Copyright © 1999, Raymond Chapman, Pauline Books & Media, Boston, MA. All Rights Reserved.

Page 145: "Into God's Care," in *Order of Service* prepared by the women of Kenya (1991), printed with permission from the Women's World Day of Prayer.

Page 146: "Christ Is with Us," in *Mysterium Fidei* by Pope Paul VI. Pauline Books & Media, Boston, MA.

Page 151: Quote from Oscar Romero in *Violence of Love* by Oscar Romero. Copyright © 1998, Plough Publishing House, Farmington, PA. All Rights Reserved.

Page 198: "Prayer to Mary," in *The Best Gift Is Love: Meditations by Mother Teresa,* compiled and edited by Sean-Patrick Lovett. Copyright © 1982 by Libreria Editrice Vaticana. Published by Servant Publications, P.O. Box 8617, Ann Arbor, Michigan 48107. Used with permission.

Page 199: "Open Us, O Lord," in *Order of Service* prepared by the women of Canada (1971). Printed with permission from The Women's World Day of Prayer.

About Blessed James Alberione

Blessed James Alberione (1884–1971), was an Italian priest and the founder of the Pauline family, including the Daughters of Saint Paul and the Society of Saint Paul. Well known for his profound spirituality and pastoral vision, Father Alberione mandated Eucharistic adoration for the institutes he founded. Despite a hectic schedule and demanding apostolic works, he daily spent four to five hours in Eucharistic prayer. Beatified on April 27, 2003, he has been called the Apostle of the New Evangelization.

To learn more about Blessed James Alberione and the Pauline Family go to www.alberione.com, or contact your nearest Pauline Books & Media Center (addresses on following page).

BOOKS & MEDIA

The Daughters of St. Paul operate book and media centers at the following addresses. Visit, call or write the one nearest you today, or find us on the World Wide Web, www.pauline.org

California
3908 Sepulveda Blvd, Culver City,
  CA 90230   310-397-8676
5945 Balboa Avenue, San Diego,
  CA 92111   858-565-9181
46 Geary Street, San Francisco,
  CA 94108   415-781-5180

Florida
145 SW 107th Avenue, Miami,
  FL 33174   305-559-6715

Hawaii
1143 Bishop Street, Honolulu,
  HI 96813   808-521-2731
Neighbor Islands call: 800-259-8463

Illinois
172 North Michigan Avenue,
  Chicago, IL 60601
  312-346-4228

Louisiana
4403 Veterans Memorial Blvd,
  Metairie, LA 70006
  504-887-7631

Massachusetts
885 Providence Hwy, Dedham,
  MA 02026   781-326-5385

Missouri
9804 Watson Road, St. Louis,
  MO 63126   314-965-3512

New Jersey
561 U.S. Route 1, Wick Plaza,
  Edison, NJ 08817   732-572-1200

New York
150 East 52nd Street, New York,
  NY 10022   212-754-1110
78 Fort Place, Staten Island, NY
  10301   718-447-5071

Pennsylvania
9171-A Roosevelt Blvd, Philadelphia,
  PA 19114   215-676-9494

South Carolina
243 King Street, Charleston, SC
  29401   843-577-0175

Tennessee
4811 Poplar Avenue, Memphis,
  TN 38117   901-761-2987

Texas
114 Main Plaza, San Antonio, TX
  78205   210-224-8101

Virginia
1025 King Street, Alexandria, VA
  22314   703-549-3806

Canada
3022 Dufferin Street, Toronto, Ontario,
  Canada M6B 3T5   416-781-9131
1155 Yonge Street, Toronto, Ontario,
  Canada M4T 1W2   416-934-3440

¡También somos su fuente para libros, videos y música en español!